Professor Errare Presents....

40 American Jackasses Worth Knowing

Professor Errare
and
S. Will Campbell

Published by Shawn Campbell

Professor Errare Presents....40 American Jackasses Worth Knowing

1st Edition

ISBN: 978-0997710564

To Herodotus, for proving to the world that fact finding is not necessarily a necessity for writing history.

And to Aaron, for still editing this book all the way through despite the questionable state in which it was in when it was handed to him.

A Note to the Reader

This book should be considered a form of parody and satire created for reasons of entertainment only. In other words, only an idiot would use this book for any type of serious citation. While Professor Errare strives to only provide factual information on the people he has deemed to be great American Jackasses, his research methods are somewhat questionable given that each person only got about an hour's worth of internet searching. As well, at times certain facts have been written about in a manner, which while entertaining, may have twisted and stretched the truth just a bit. If you find anything in this book interesting Professor Errare strongly encourages you to do your own research. The internet represents the greatest source of knowledge in human history, so maybe try using it for more than cat videos and porn, and of course, cat porn videos.

It's important to remember while reading this book that every single one of us is a jackass in one way or another. However, being included in this book doesn't necessarily mean that a person is a full blown jackass. Sometimes, as you will soon discover, the story is actually that everyone else around them is a jackass. However, you have to call a book something, so let's not shit ourselves over semantics.

Finally, Professor Errare would like to apologize for not including a statistically accurate number of women and minority groups in this book. After plodding his way through the army of old white men who made up the presidents, he did his best to create more diversity with this book. However, while he found some, they were far outnumbered by old white dudes. Unfortunately, it takes not being oppressed to become a truly great jackass.

As a final statement, the clever reader will probably notice that a good chunk of these jackasses lived in the nineteenth century. This is not to say that we haven't had plenty of jackasses in modern times, only that the nineteenth century was a time when a jackass could truly reach their full jackass potential.

Okay, now that we have the please don't sue me stuff out of the way. Here we go....

#1 Zebulon Pike
Lewis And Clark Were Pansies

If you really think about it, the Lewis and Clark expedition was basically a bunch of guys who just paddled some boats on a couple of rivers and almost starved to death a few times because they were idiots. Now if you want to talk about a top notch expedition of exploration, then you need to consider Zebulon Pike.

Zeb was a military man who spent most of his early career on the frontier, exploring the headwaters of the Mississippi and whatnot. In 1806, Zeb's superior office, a chubby bastard named General James Wilkinson, ordered the then 27 year old Zeb to lead an expedition to explore the Red River in the present day states of Kansas, Nebraska, and Colorado, which had recently been acquired via the Louisiana Purchase. It was the usual "draw some maps and make contact with the locals" kind of expedition with a little "why not secretly enter what was then Spanish territory and just look around a bit" thrown in.

Zeb's first task was to return a bunch of native hostage back to their tribe. This was the only part of the expedition that went well. Soon after, he came upon a group of Spanish explorers, and much like what you did with your high school prom date, decided that it would be best if he just kind of started stalking them for weeks on end. This mostly involved acting casual yet surprised whenever they ran into each other at the mall or while entering native villages as soon as the Spanish left in order to demand that they take down the Spanish flag and hang the U.S. flag up in its place. Again, much like your high school prom date, Zeb eventually got bored with these shenanigans, so instead decided to climb a 14,000 foot mountain for no particular reason. Zeb failed, but they later named the mountain Pike's Peak in his honor. Today you can drive to the top of this very same mountain in your car. Following the failed and pointless mountain climbing attempts, Zeb and his expedition became hopelessly lost for months, wandering around in a giant circle which ended exactly where it had started. Unperturbed, Zeb then pushed his exhausted and starving men south into Spanish territory, leaving behind anyone who was unable to keep up.

Soon after entering Spanish territory, Zeb and his men were arrested by the Spanish authorities. The Spanish had known the whole time that Zeb was coming because his superior, General Wilkerson, in a convoluted plot to create his own country west of the Mississippi, was secretly a spy for Spain. Zeb and his men, now prisoners, were taken deeper into Mexico where a party was thrown in their honor in every town they passed through, because who doesn't enjoy a good party? During these celebrations the Spanish authorities made the discovery that Zeb was bumbling idiot, and feeling bad for him, let him go and escorted him back to the United States with full military honors. Most of the rest of the expedition remained imprisoned in Mexico, some not returning to the United States for years.

Following his ill fated expedition, Zeb continued on with his military career, generally fumbling his way from one position to the next. During the War of 1812 he was a part of the U.S. invasion of Canada where he died when a large rock, propelled by an even larger explosion, smashed his head in.

#2 William Walker
Filibusters Were Once Kind of Cool

Few people combined the expansionist ideal of American Manifest Destiny with the crazy notion that somebody can do anything that they put their mind to quite like William Walker. Born into a wealthy plantation family in Tennessee, William attended school at several universities in the U.S., Scotland, and Germany, before getting his medical degree at the age 19. He soon set up his own practice, but it did not last long. William found practicing medicine boring so he moved to New Orleans where he received a law degree and founded his own newspaper. He also met and fell in love with a deaf mute woman named Helen Martin. However, before they could marry, the bride to be died of yellow fever. Heart broken, William moved to San Francisco and took up the synergistic hobbies of heavy drinking and getting shot in duels.

By age 29, William had already tried being a doctor, lawyer, and newspaper editor, so he decided that his next logical career move should be president. Not wanting to bother with the horse shit of campaigns and elections, William instead convinced 45 drunken assholes to invade Mexico. William and his drunken personal army conquered the Baja Peninsula, which was quite easy given that nobody really wanted to live in such a god forsaken place anyway. William called his new country the Republic of Sonora, which was kind of a stupid name given that he wasn't in Sonora. He also legalized slavery in his new, illegal republic, because if you're going to go crazy you might as well go all the way.

However, William was better at making drunken speeches than actually being a general. It was soon discovered that he had made the strategic mistake of not bringing any food with him, and so when the Mexican army arrived, he was forced to retreat back to the U.S. after only six months of being president.

As soon as William got back to San Francisco he was arrested for waging an illegal war and put on trial. However, given that the general American sentiment at the time was "fuck Mexico" he was acquitted by the jury after only eight minutes of deliberation. William hung out in San Francisco for about a year and a half before hearing of a civil war in Nicaragua. Sensing opportunity, he gathered a new army of 60 random drunks, headed south to the small Central American nation, and promptly seized control of the government. Not happy with just owning Nicaragua, he then tried to invade Costa Rica, a move which resulted in a war not just with Costa Rica, but also with Honduras, Guatemala, El Salvador, and the British and U.S. Navies. This did not go well for William, who after 19 months as de facto president of Nicaragua, burned the country's capital to the ground and surrendered to the U.S. Navy. The U.S. Navy took him to New York where the people threw him a parade.

Later that year, William raised a third army and tried to invade Nicaragua again, but the U.S. Navy arrested him and promptly told him to cut it out with the shenanigans. William spent the next three years writing a book about his exploits and getting drunk at fancy rich people parties. At age 36 a group of settlers approached him about setting up an independent country on a small group of islands owned by Honduras. William eagerly agreed and set out to become a president once again with a small group of drunks. Upon arrival in Honduras he took over a small government building but was quickly arrested by the British navy who handed him over to the Honduran government. The government of Honduras, tired of William's bullshit, put him in front of a firing squad.

#3 Frederic Tudor
The Ice King

In the dark days before refrigeration was invented, people in the tropics had no way to enjoy icy drinks. That's right., no margaritas, no daiquiris, and definitely no pina coladas. At least, that was until Freddy, over dressed in his old timey heavy wool clothes, visited the Caribbean and sweatily decided the lack of ice was bull shit. Hence, one of the great American entrepreneurs set out on his journey to greatness.

Freddy was a man of the early 19th century, a stern unsmiling demeanor wrapped in a halo of curly hair and massive mutton chops. Born into a wealthy Boston family, Freddy spent the summer of his 22nd year much like the rich kids of today, in the Caribbean sweating his balls off. However, unlike today's entitled youths, the experience actually gave Freddy an idea. Specifically, he realized that relaxing in the Caribbean would be a lot nicer if they could get some cool drinks up in that shit. The Caribbean needed ice, and his homeland of New England had too much of it. Why not just load a shit ton of ice on a boat and ship it on down?   Now if at this point you are saying to yourself, "because ice melts, stupid," congratulations, you have already given it more thought than Freddy did. Running back up to New England, he soon sent down sent down his first frosty shipment. Mysteriously, half of his first cargo of ice disappeared. The remainder was sold at a loss or melted whilst sitting on the sweltering dock.

Now at this point most people would have had a good laugh at how silly they had been and call it good. Not Freddy. Undeterred, he doubled down, sending more ships filled with frozen water into the hot tropic sun, losing money with each vessel to the point that he was thrown in debtor's prison a couple of times. For those not in the know, debtor's prison was where you got sent if you were unable to pay your debts, which is a surefire way of making sure you will probably never make enough money to pay back said debts. Still undeterred, the moment Freddy got out, he borrowed more money and set out for Cuba in yet another vessel filled with ice, the police literally just missing him at the wharf.

While Freddy may have been a bit of a stubborn idiot, he was also a perseverant one. Over the years of literally beating his head against the wall, he learned to adopt newer and better technologies. Ice was coated in sawdust and straw, and ice houses were built at Caribbean ports. After 19 years of losing money, Freddy quite suddenly became a success. Ships carrying ice from New England started sailing regularly to the Caribbean, the Deep South, and even as far as India, where riots broke out when people, many of whom had never seen ice before, saw their miraculous purchase literally melt in their hands.

Freddy celebrated his success the way most successful men do, by marrying a woman 30 years his junior and pumping out a bunch of heirs. He also tried his hand at more conventional industries, such as fruit and coffee imports, but failed at both miserably. Ice was to remain his chilled bread and butter for the rest of his life. The export of ice from New England to the rest of the world rapidly became one of the United States' top exports. Freddy died in 1864 at the age of 80, just as the first early refrigerators were being invented.

#4 John O'Neill
Not Good at Irish Patriotism

The mid-nineteenth century was not a good time for Ireland, what with the heavy-handed rule of the British and the whole potato famine thing genocidally killing all sorts of folks. It was these conditions that forced Johnny O to flee to the United States at the age of 14, a habit not unheard of amongst his fellow Irishman. However, things were not much better in the good old U.S. of A., what with the rampant racism against Irish immigrants and whatnot. Finding the jobs available to a young Irishman in the U.S. less than satisfactory, young Johnny O joined the military and became a cavalry officer, fighting in both the Utah War and Civil War. Following the Civil War, Johnny O found himself out of a job, which was when the Fenian Brotherhood found him.

The Fenian Brotherhood was a group of Irish patriots, or terrorists depending on who you're asking, who were busily training men and stockpiling weapons in the U.S. to use some day to free Ireland from British rule. Johnny O loved the group's passion, but took issue with the fact that they were long on preparation and short on actually doing anything. Using some interesting "outside the box" thinking Johnny O decided that the best course of action would be for the Fenian's to invade Canada, which would then somehow result in the British granting Ireland its independence. Nobody was sure exactly how this plan was going to work, but the thought of actually doing something proved very popular, so the Fenian's just kind of went with it.

In 1866, Johnny O led 1,200 Fenians in an invasion of Canada. Which was less of an invasion, and more walking 10 miles across the border and occupying a small town of 800 people called Ridgeway, Ontario. The Canadians, not really sure what to make of the whole thing, sent a small detachment of troops to check things out, who promptly had their asses handed to them by the Fenians, most of whom were Civil War veterans. Following their victory, the Fenians sat around for a few days, waiting for Ireland to become free, eventually growing bored and returning to the United States. Despite having accomplished little, Johnny O was declared a hero.

Hot off of his first so-called success, Johnny O waited four years and then led a second invasion of Canada, but this time in Quebec, because obviously the British probably cared more about the French speaking part of Canada than they did the English speaking part. The invasion did not start out well. Johnny O was arrested trying to cross the border, and soon after his army of a few hundred men, leaderless and confused, were easily trounced by the Canadian military. Johnny O was sentenced to two years in prison, but President Useless S. Grant, finding the whole thing rather ridiculous, pardoned him after only a few months.

A free man again, Johnny O decided that the best course of action was to invade Canada for a third time. This time he targeted Manitoba, mostly because almost nobody lived there at the time. The third invasion went worse than the second. Johnny O and his army, consisting of a couple dozen men, apparently none of whom knew how to read a map, invaded U.S. territory. The Canadian military responded by marching into the United States and beating the ever living snot out of the Fenians, who were then arrested by U.S. authorities. When questioned, Johnny O claimed that he and his men had just been going north to start an Irish colony. The U.S. government, finding the whole thing ridiculous and really wanting nothing to do with any of it, let Johnny O and his men go.

After the failure of the third invasion, Johnny O finally accepted that invading Canada would probably not result in a free Ireland. Not sure what else to do, he worked the rest of his life on what he apparently thought was the next best thing, promoting Irish immigration to Nebraska.

#5 Lloyd Olsen
The Man with the Famous Chicken

In the 1940's Lloyd Olsen was just a poor farmer trying his best to scratch a living out of dirt in Colorado, but all that changed when he met Mike the magic chicken. The story begins when Lloyd found out his mother-in-law was coming for a visit. Knowing that the woman was an avid lover of chicken neck, as all classy women are, Lloyd went out to kill a chicken for the pot, aiming the axe to make sure to save as much neck as possible. However, after the head fell to the ground, Lloyd was left with a bit of a surprise. The chicken, despite its decapitation, was still alive. Not only was it still alive, but it was still walking around and doing its pathetic best to peck and preen. Lloyd, seeing that this chicken was something special and being a man who knew an opportunity when he saw one, promptly took it into town and started betting people beers that he had a living headless chicken.

The chicken, soon after named Mike for some reason, was possibly the most lucky, or unlucky depending on how you look at it, chicken in the world. The axe blade had only cut away half of Mike's brain, which proved to be the half chickens really don't apparently need. Lloyd cared for his new best friend by shoving milk and small pieces of corn down Mike's esophagus, and clearing away mucus with a syringe. Mike didn't seem to mind the arrangement, probably because he was a lobotomized fucking chicken. Lloyd took Mike to the nearest university where he was poked and prodded until the assorted professors all agreed that Mike was indeed alive. The professors then tried to replicate Mike's creation, purely in the interest of science, but only ended up with a bunch of dead chickens. It was at this time that Lloyd met a bit of a shyster named Hope Wade who convinced him that there were better ways to use Mike besides scamming local drunks for free beer.

So how does a man make money off a headless chicken in the 1940's? Why by joining the side show circuit of course. TV hadn't been invented yet and returning veterans from the most horrible war in history needed something to distract them from their PTSD. Lloyd and Mike crisscrossed the country, showing off Mike for a quarter a head (around $2.75 in today's cash). Mike became a nationwide celebrity, appearing in major magazines and ruffling feathers with the rich and famous. Lloyd, being a more down to earth soul, used the money to buy a hay baler, two tractors, and a pickup truck. Fan mail from across the country came in, including one that called Lloyd a Nazi for some reason. People in the 1940's took their chickens very seriously.

After 18 months of touring, the gravy train that was Mike the magic chicken unfortunately came to an end. While staying at a seedy motel, as all sideshow acts are required to do, Mike choked on a piece of corn and died. Lloyd, horrified by his loss, told everyone he had sold Mike and then tossed the out the body on the side of the road to be devoured by coyotes. With Mike gone, Lloyd went back to his simple life of being a farmer, only occasionally bothered by people bringing chickens, six packs of beer, and a hope that there might be a chance that Lloyd could repeat the miracle that was Mike.

#6 Homer Plessy
Civil Rights Activist and Railroad Stooge

It should come as no surprise that the late nineteenth century was not a very good time to be a black person in the United States, but apparently the state of Louisiana did not feel that things were bad enough. In 1890 the state legislature passed a new law requiring the railroads to have separate passenger cars for whites and blacks for reasons that can only be described as super racist. Unsurprisingly, this new law pissed off the civil rights activists of the time. More surprising was the fact that it also pissed off the various railroad companies that operated in Louisiana. No, not because the railroad owners loved the idea of justice and equality, but because having to keep everyone separate would require more passenger cars which would cut into their profits. The two groups got together and what resulted was one of the strangest combinations of greed and social justice in American history.

The activists and the railroads, working together, came up with a convoluted plot to force the challenging of the law in the court system. The plot involved having a stooge get arrested for sitting in the whites only passenger car. The stooge they picked was a man by the name of Homer. Homer was a middle class shoe maker who was a bit of a strange pick given that in his photo he resembles a long lost son of President Garfield's.

However, despite his outward appearance, Homer was 1/8 black, which made him more than enough black for the people of the time to treat like shit. Being 1/8th black made Homer, in the old timey racist speak of the time, a quadroon, which would have been a great name for a store bought cookie, you know, if it wasn't already a super racist term.

Homer, on a hot summer day purchased a train ticket, climbed aboard the white's only rail car, which nobody batted an eye at because again he looked like James Garfield's progeny, and then promptly told the conductor that he was 1/8 black. The conductor, not letting appearances get in the way of his racism, freaked the fuck out and tried to throw Homer out of the car, which resulted in what the newspapers of the time called a severe altercation. Luckily for all involved, there was a private investigator on board the train, who had also been hired by the railroad, who promptly arrested Homer for breaking the law, because that was something private investigators could do back then. From there, the plan went along swimmingly. Homer's case, defended by railroad funded lawyers, worked its way through the legal system until finally reaching the U.S. Supreme Court four years later.

The arguments before the Supreme Court were viewed as rather elementary by both sides. On Homer's side the argument was that the law was stupid and racist. On the state of Louisiana's side, the argument was that god wanted Louisiana to keep whites and blacks from mixing, which was pretty difficult to prove given that god could not be called upon to testify. Despite this, in the end the Supreme Court, which was entirely made up of old frumpy white men, found in a 7-1 decision that the Louisiana law was about public policy, not racism, and that it was A-Okay as long as the passenger cars for the two groups were relatively the same. This decision opened the door for 68 years of super racist Jim Crow laws, which made things decidedly worse for blacks in the United States, and less importantly, hurt the railroads' profit margins. So yeah, it was all pretty fucked up.

#7 Mary Mallon
The Woman Who Was Never Sick a Day in Her Life

Getting sick sucks, but you know what sucks more? Having your body be a literal germ factory that infects anyone that comes near you and becoming the quite literal boogeyman of the early 20th century. That was the sad fate of Typhoid Mary.

TM was born to a poor family in Ireland, and like many young Irish of the time, immigrated to New York City at the tender age of 15 to find better opportunities. For TM, those opportunities involved cooking for rich people, a job she proved amazingly good at despite thinking hand washing was highfalutin tom foolery. However, while people found her food very delicious, everyone TM worked for kept coming down with typhoid fever. Over a seven year period she worked for eight different families, and all but one saw the majority of their households fall ill, which for a number of people also involved dying. Eventually, this strange set of circumstances led to an investigation by a doctor with a wealth of medical knowledge, but fairly shitty people skills.

It didn't take long for the good doctor, being a man with the basic skill of pattern recognition, to figure out that TM was the common denominator. The doctor went to

TM's place of work and told her she was giving everyone typhoid, a fact she found hard to believe given she was healthy as a horse. The doctor, lacking tact, then asked if he could have a stool sample. Not enjoying being harassed by what appeared to her to be a quack with a fecal fetish, TM grabbed a carving knife, started cursing like a drunken sailor, and chased the doctor out the door. The doctor, a persistent fellow, proceeded to harass TM for several weeks, demanding she hand over her poop. When this tactic didn't work, he brought in the police, and TM was summarily arrested, after putting up a huge curse laden fight, and placed into quarantine on an isolated island in the East River.

TM was held in isolation on that island for three years, during which time she was forced to turn over her poop on a weekly basis. Finding a large amount of typhoid in her gall bladder, the medical experts suggested removing it. TM refused and instead started personally sending more poop samples to a private lab for analysis. When the private lab tests came back negative she sued the government and lost, but was later released due to public outcry over her forced isolation. However, as part of her release agreement she had to agree to quit her career as a cook. TM gladly agreed, returned to New York City, changed her name, and went back to cooking delicious meals with her very dirty hands.

TM thought she was doing nothing wrong, because again, she felt she was healthy as a horse. Perhaps to prove her point, five years after her release she took a job cooking at a maternity hospital, where she was caught because pretty much everybody got typhoid, which is not a plus in a maternity hospital. Tiring of TM's shit, literally, the city medical experts quarantined her back on the isolated island in the East River. TM there, mostly alone except for a dog and the occasional visitor, for the next 23 years. During this time, for god only knows what reason, she was allowed to work at the hospital on the island in the laboratory, but only under, what can be assumed, close hand washing supervision. TM died at age 69 in 1938. Four years later they invented antibiotics, reducing typhoid from a deadly disease to a minor distasteful annoyance.

#8 Sylvester Graham
White Bread Makes You Lustful

Today, fad diets are all the rage with people making all sorts of wacky claims in their quest for a magic elixir for better health. But back in the early nineteenth century people didn't give such things much thought; food was just food, at least until Sylvester hit the scene.

Sylvester was a Presbyterian minister who had taken the cloth because he was basically good at nothing else. Like all ministers, Sylvester needed some kind of evil to preach against in order to get his congregation all riled up into a holy frenzy. Unlike other ministers, Sylvester chose white bread as his devil. At the time, white bread was a fairly new concept having only been recently invented. Thought of as being better than traditional whole wheat bread, it was rapidly gaining dominance as the bread preferred by the genteel to shove into their mouth holes. Sylvester wholeheartedly did not agree. He believed that the good old whole wheat bread was healthier, which is scientifically correct, though not to the point that makes what happened next make any damn sense at all. You see, claiming that white bread was just somewhat unhealthier than whole wheat bread doesn't really make for all that exciting of a sermon, so Sylvester decided to spice it up a little.

According to Sylvester's rants from the pulpit, not only was white bread unhealthy, it was so unhealthy that it caused people to have excessive sexual desires, which every old timey person knew was definitely not good for you. Even worse, all that bread inspired lust resulted in masturbation, which was the root cause of blindness, insanity, and early death. Well, you can bet your ass this got those old timey people's attention, and so the first fad diet was born. Sylvester, amazed by the power of his own sermon, of course did not take advantage of his new found fame and following. Just kidding, he kicked the crazy up to 10.

Now if you're a minister who has started the first widely successful fad diet, what would you do? If you didn't answer turn it into a cult, you just aren't thinking big enough. Seeing his success with white bread, Sylvester doubled down in every way possible. Not only was white bread unhealthy, but so was meat, spices of any kind, and alcohol. These items had to cleared from the diet to avoid the evils of masturbation, which later grew to the evils of sex all together, which then became the evils of any excitement whatsoever. People ate it up like it was wholesome white bread, and the followers of Sylvester's diet shifted from annoying jerks to crazed religious zealots who creatively called themselves Grahamites.

Now the average Grahamite was a fairly bland person, what with all the rules limiting excitement of any kind. The most exciting part of their day was the cult ordered daily brushing of their teeth. The problem was it was hard to find food that was bland enough to keep them from getting over stimulated. To help, Sylvester invented the blandest food possible, the Graham cracker. That's right, this staple of your childhood was invented by a man for his anti-masturbation health cult. Of course, the whole thing came crashing down when, despite eating healthy and avoiding sex of any kind, Sylvester died at the not quite venerable age of 57. Just kidding, the cult lasted for another 30 years before finally fading into obscurity.

#9 Annie Edson Taylor
The Queen of The Mist

Annie, a very prim and proper sort who once yelled at a child for eating peanuts in front of a lady, was born into a privileged existence. Her father was the wealthy owner of a flour mill who saved enough money to sustain his family in prosperity for years after his premature death. Annie used her inheritance to learn to be a teacher and soon after married a nice young man of similar upbringing. It was at this point that everything went pretty much to shit for her. The couple had a child that died in infancy and soon after her husband was killed in the Civil War. Annie, now a young widow, did exactly what many young women do today when their lives go into the crapper. She traveled the country, taking odd teaching jobs to support herself, and eventually opened a dance studio which failed not long after its grand opening.

As Annie approached her 63rd birthday she faced the terrible reality that she was dead broke and getting older by the minute. The prospect of being a penniless invalid scared the living hell out of her. It scared her so much that she decided that her only hope was to do something crazy to make herself famous, which even back then wasn't all that solid of a plan. In this day and age, a woman with no talent who wants to be famous can just make a sex tape. However, given that movie film was still in its infancy at the time, and that probably nobody would want to watch her so-called film even if it wasn't, Annie decided that her best option was to go over Niagara Falls in a pickle barrel. It was a feat no one had even imagined until that moment, which didn't seem to bother Annie one bit. Hiring a manager by the name of Tussy to hype the event, she began making preparations to go over the falls on October 24, 1901, the date of her 63rd birthday.

Annie was not entirely a crazy person. First, she made sure her barrel was specially outfitted with harnesses and cushions. Second, she put her cat in the barrel and sent it over the falls a few days before just to make sure it would work. The cat came out fine, and apparently being the calmest house cat in the world, even posed for a picture soon after. Finally, she told everyone she was 44 for some reason, because apparently old timey people considered a 44 year old woman going over a waterfall as being more amazing than a 63 year old one for some reason. When the big day came, Annie climbed into her barrel in front of a crowd of curious onlookers. The barrel was then towed out to the middle of the river and set loose. She went over the falls and disappeared into the water and mist. Twenty minutes later it bobbed to the surface downriver. Annie survived, intact and unharmed.

Unfortunately, the feat did little to change Annie's luck. Soon after the event, her manager Tussy stole her barrel and started touring it around the country with a younger woman who pretended to be Annie. Without her barrel, Annie was forced to rely on her own charisma, which was about as magnetic as drying paint. What little money she did make in the preceding months of her five minutes of fame was spent paying private investigators to track down Tussy and the barrel, which none ever managed to do. Annie spent the rest of her life surviving by running a souvenir stand, posing for pictures, and even working as a fortune teller for a time. When she died at the age of 83 she was completely broke and what few admirers she had were forced to raise money to erect a headstone.

#10 Tisquantum
When Life Gives You Lemons It Sucks

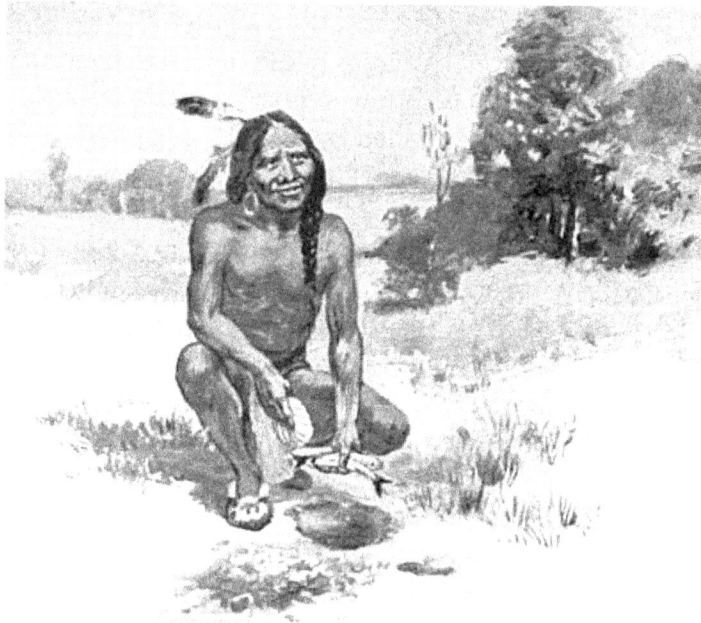

Tisquantum was a Native American who lived in New England in the early 17th century. The white people, for reasons that can only be described as being total assholes, called him Squanto.

Squanto was a member of the Patuxet tribe of the Wampanoag Confederacy, a group of native tribes which controlled modern day Massachusetts, Connecticut, Rhode Island, and Long Island. Squanto had a pretty good early childhood, living with his parents and hanging out with his peeps. This changed when Squanto saw his first white men at the age of 10. The white men, explorers from England, seeing Squanto just hanging out on the beach, collected him as though he was some strange type of bug, and took him back to England. When Squanto arrived in England he was given as a gift to the explorers' boss, because gifting people was totally okay back then. The boss, delighted with his new acquisition, taught Squanto English so he could act as an interpreter for future voyages.

After four years in England, Squanto was made part of a new expedition and taken back to New England, where he promptly escaped and started making his way home. However, before he could make it, another English explorer re-captured him, took him to Spain, and tried to sell him into slavery for around $3,500 in today's money. Luckily, some Catholic friars rescued Squanto before he could be forced into explicit servitude, rather than the implicit servitude he had already been putting up with. Unluckily, the friars then forced Squanto to become a Catholic. After hanging out with the friars for a bit, Squanto made his way back to England where he worked for a shipbuilder, and after a few years, got himself on a voyage to Newfoundland. However, when he tried to leave, the English explorers just kind of laughed, probably in a very snide manner, and took him back to England.

A full nine years after being captured, Squanto finally boarded a ship that took him home to New England to stay. Unfortunately, upon arrival, he discovered that pretty much everyone he had ever known had been killed by a plague of smallpox brought by some white dudes the previous year. In fact, it's estimated that up to 90 percent of the Wampanoag Confederacy died during the period of Squanto's capture. Not sure what else to do, Squanto mostly spent the next two years hanging out in his abandoned village and occasionally visiting distant relatives from other nearby tribes. It was around this time that the Pilgrims, yes, those Pilgrims, showed up on the scene. The Pilgrims, who were long on religious convictions, but short on survival skills, nearly starved their first winter in Massachusetts. Squanto, feeling bad for them, which is impressive considering his life so far, never mind the fact that white people at the time weren't big on bathing, taught the Pilgrims how to grow corn.

For some reason, the Pilgrims and the surviving Wampanoag did not get along. Squanto, thanks to his English skills, and his ability to put up with the Pilgrims' terrible body odor, became an ambassador between the two groups, promoting peaceful co-existence. This position did not prove popular with everyone. A renegade group of Wampanoag kidnapped Squanto with plans to kill him, but he was rescued by a group of Pilgrims. Soon after, while on a peace mission, Squanto fell sick, probably due to being poisoned, and died. His efforts won the Wampanoag fifty years of peace. Peace in this case meant that the natives suffered a series of small pox epidemics and slowly got kicked off their lands by the growing number of white people.

#11 Hugh Glass
Better Than the Movie

Hugh was born to perfectly normal immigrant parents in late eighteenth century Pennsylvania. Finding being normal boring as hell, Hugh left home at a young age and bummed around the frontier for a decade or so, which at the time ended at the Mississippi River, doing random low paying jobs to get by. This lifestyle came to an abrupt end when at age 33 he was captured by a notorious pirate and forced to join the buccaneer's crew. Hugh made the most of this turn of events and spent two years as a pirate. He eventually returned to land, by deciding to jump off the ship and swim two miles to shore, where he was promptly captured by the Pawnee tribe, who burned his business partner alive, but spared Hugh after he gave the tribe's chief some fancy red dye. Again, just going along with it, Hugh then married a Pawnee woman and settled in with the tribe that had only recently tried to murder him.

After two years of marital bliss, Hugh decided that marriage just didn't suit him, so he left his wife and returned to civilization. He ended up joining a large group of fur trappers and traveled to the Rocky Mountains where they were attacked by another tribe called the Arikara. Soon after this attack, Hugh, who was then forty years old, got himself

26

mauled by a grizzly bear. Convinced Hugh was going to die, the fur trappers decided to leave John Fitzgerald and a young Jim Bridger to bury him while the rest went on their way. Fitzgerald and Bridger, rightfully scared as shit of the Arikara, put the still alive Hugh in a shallow grave, took his gun and knife, and hastily left. Things did not work as planned. Hugh, despite being all torn to shit, didn't die. Instead he dragged his maggot covered corpse over 200 miles to the nearest American settlement, arriving six weeks later. During the trip he mostly lived off of roots and berries. As well, a friendly native also sewed a buffalo skin to his wounded back, though that might have just been some kind of elaborate joke.

Hugh was a little perturbed at being left to die in the middle of nowhere, and spent his time recuperating plotting intricate revenge schemes. After regaining his health, he set out to find Bridger and Fitzgerald. After several months of tracking, Hugh managed to find Bridger first, but decided to forgive him because Bridger was only 19 years old, apparently making him too young to know that abandoning people to die was the wrong thing to do. It took Hugh over a year to track down Fitzgerald. When Hugh finally found him, Fitzgerald had joined the U.S. Army. Unable to kill Fitzgerald, Hugh settled with just getting his rifle back and threatening to kill Fitzgerald if he ever left the Army.

His revenge sort of complete, Hugh took his reclaimed rifle and went back to his old job of fur trapping. His luck at this occupation continued to be poor. Hugh was attacked and wounded several more times by the natives over the next ten years. This culminated, when at age 50, Hugh's old friends the Arikara ambushed him, shot him several times, and then scalped him, finally finishing him off. Not long after, another group of fur trappers caught the Arikara responsible, and after seeing they had Hugh's beloved rifle, burned them alive. It goes without saying that the Old West in the early nineteenth century was an incredibly shitty place to live.

#12 H.H. Holmes
What the Hell Holy Shit

The 1893 Chicago World's Fair was an amazing celebration of the American gilded age. It was an exposition of firsts. First movie theater, first Ferris Wheel, first Pabst Blue Ribbon, and America's first serial killer.

H.H. was born Herman Mudgett, a moniker he abandoned for obvious reasons. His terrible name aside, Herman did not have a happy childhood. When he wasn't getting violently beaten by his alcoholic father, he was getting tortured and bullied by his future alcoholic classmates. Herman dealt with his problems by dissecting small animals. I think we can all see where this one is going. He attended university to become a medical doctor, an endeavor he paid for by using cadavers from the university in complicated life insurance schemes. This did not sit well with his first wife for some reason, so she left, a fact that didn't bother Herman in the least. He soon got remarried, without ever getting officially divorced, and started traveling the country, taking on odd jobs and murdering a few children here and there. Herman's new wife was apparently the most oblivious woman in history.

After a few years of random murder, Herman, finding himself in Chicago, decided to shift homicides from a hobby to a full on industry. He secured a city block on which he built a massive edifice that was supposedly a hotel, but would later be called the Murder Castle. The Murder Castle was built over several years with no workman allowed to be part of its construction for more than a few weeks at a time. It was a maze of hallways and false doors. Air tight and sound proof rooms provided the perfect spots for various types of murder. Strangulation, asphyxiation, poison, and starvation just to name a few. In the basement Herman set up his own personal laboratory where he dissected and did away with the bodies using acid, lime, and incineration. The entire monstrosity was funded by a combination of life insurance scams and the selling of skeletons across the country to doctors' offices and universities.

Herman's second wife must have been the most oblivious woman in history. Not only did he run a murder factory right under her nose, he also fueled it by seducing women from across the country, luring them into his lair. Woman after woman fell to the charms of Herman. Several of these mistresses stayed in his hotel for months before being dealt with. Herman even got married for a third time, even though he was still legally married to his first two wives, though in the grand scheme of things, his penchant for bigamy probably wasn't that big of a deal what with the wanton murder and all. Herman's "business" reached its high point during the Chicago World's Fair. With thousands of people flocking to the city, many couldn't be that picky when it came to available hotel rooms.

Soon after the end of the World's Fair, Herman was forced to flee to avoid the police. His second wife probably just thought he was leaving for cigarettes or something. Herman tried to stay low, but couldn't keep himself from running a few non-murdery horse swindles and life insurance scams. Growing bored, Herman killed his only friend, kidnapped three of the man's children, and then led his widow on what he thought was probably a merry chase across the U.S. and Canada. This chase of course ended with the children getting murdered, because at this point how else could it end. Herman was soon captured, tried for several of his murders, and hanged. It's estimated that he killed up to 200 people. His last words basically hinted that he was probably the devil.

#13 Lincoln Beachey
One Crazy Son of A Bitchy

Lincoln was a chubby lonely kid born close to the end of the 19th century. Being socially inept, the young Lincoln decided on a slightly different method for making friends. That method involved doing crazy stunts like riding a bike with no brakes down San Francisco's famous hilly streets. By the time Lincoln was a teenager, bike riding had become boring, so he set his focus on becoming an aviator. This was not an easy task, given that airplanes had just been invented two years prior, which really made it unlikely that anybody was going to let some crazy seventeen year old kid pilot one. Lincoln had to settle for the next best thing: being a test pilot for experimental dirigibles, which involved sitting in a basket under a huge balloon full of hydrogen gas. It was exactly as safe as it sounds. After five years of somehow not dying in a fiery explosion or ground impact, Lincoln finally got his big break while attending an air show where the pilot of a bi-plane became too sick to fly. Despite having no idea what he was doing, Lincoln volunteered. He flew the plane up 3,000 feet and promptly put it into a death spiral. By some miracle Lincoln managed to land the plane, and with that, an American hero was born.

Lincoln went to work for Glenn Curtis as a stunt pilot, again, with almost no flying experience. Lincoln, nonplussed, taught himself how to fly by crashing three planes. At first Lincoln just repeatedly did his death spiral maneuver, but when that got old he moved on to racing trains in his plane, flying under low bridges, and down Niagara Falls. He was the first pilot to perform figure 8's and the first to do vertical drops to achieve terminal velocity. When he got tired of flying down, he flew straight up, setting altitude records above 11,000 feet. Lincoln then performed the first night flight, dropping flares and noise makers over Los Angeles for a gag, and the first indoor flight, taking off and landing inside the same building. All of this is even more impressive considering this was a time when planes were made of wood and canvas, and that Lincoln was doing all of his flying in a business suit. In 1914, 17 million people came to his airshows, 20 percent of the whole U.S. population at the time.

When Lincoln wasn't acting crazy, he was playing pranks. These included dressing like a woman and then flying erratically to make fun of fellow aviator Blanche Scott, dive bombing the White House, and blowing up a replica of a U.S. battleship. However, things weren't all laughs. Lincoln's fame as a crazy man who flew airplanes straight at the ground garnered a lot of copycats, many of whom strangely died in airplane crashes. Feeling guilty, Lincoln retired from flying and tried his hand at selling real estate. This lasted a few months, until another aviator performed the first loop de loop. Horrified that someone else was doing new tricks before he did, Lincoln got back into the biz, painted his name in huge letters on his plane, and not only started doing multiple loops, but also started flying upside down.

The remainder of Lincoln's career largely involved doing loop after loop, sometimes as many as eighty in a row. However, loops didn't pay the bills, so he also raced his plane against the famous race car driver Barney Oldfield, letting the car win sometimes just to keep things interesting. Lincoln was forced into retirement for a second time in 1915 when at age 28 he plowed an experimental monoplane into San Francisco Bay. Lincoln survived the crash, but drowned before rescuers could reach him. Across the country, children mourned him by making up a jump rope song about what a crazy idiot he was.

#14 Sam Hill
What in Sam Hill?

Scatter-brained, simple, and manic-depressive. They just don't make business magnates like Sam Hill anymore.

Sam was born to a Quaker family which moved to Minnesota to avoid the Civil War. After attending Harvard University, Sam set himself up at a law practice and made a name for himself by suing railroads. One railroad owner, James Hill (unrelated) rather tired of Sam's antics, solved the issue by hiring Sam and making him an executive. Sam thanked his benefactor by marrying the man's daughter Mary, who was thereafter known as Mary Hill Hill. Thanks to his fat railroad paycheck, and a generous wedding gift from his father-in-law, Sam was thrust into the highfalutin world of the American gilded age, rubbing shoulders with millionaires, taking vacations to Europe, and becoming quite the man about town in Minneapolis.

As the start of the 20th century rolled around Sam got rather tired of railroads and his interests switched to electric companies. He moved to Seattle and purchased the local light and gas company. His wife and two children followed, but after six months they moved back to Minneapolis. Sam didn't mind a bit. His wife was becoming an invalid, his daughter was nutty enough to get locked in a mental institution, and his son was the worst kind of rich kid lay about. Sam built himself a mansion in Seattle, which he paid for by doubling gas rates, and soon after sold his electric company and successfully invested in the stock market, netting him enough money to try whatever batshit crazy idea entered his head. It was at this time that Sam became obsessed with roads, traveling the world to study them, and pushing Oregon and Washington to build a highway up the Columbia River Gorge. This probably had nothing to do with the fact that he had purchased a large tract of land in Eastern Washington along the Columbia River that was pretty much nothing but rock and steep hillside. Oregon in the end gave in, building a highway with more aesthetic than practical value.

Though he was estranged from his wife, Sam was never lonely thanks to an army of mistresses. Three of these women became pregnant, an issue Sam solved by marrying them off to random acquaintances so his offspring wouldn't be considered bastards. When his favorite mistress became pregnant, Sam built her a mansion and married her off to his cousin, but of course kept sleeping with her. Sam, growing tired of roads, moved on to telephones, starting an unsuccessful telephone company in Portland. He then spent World War I riding a train through Europe and Russia. Sam claimed he was spying for the U.S. government, but actually he was just being a crazy rich guy. Following the war, Sam decided to build a bunch of monuments just because he could. The first was a concrete version of Stonehenge built on his butt fuck nowhere property in Eastern Washington to commemorate three local men who had died in World War I. The second was a massive arch, called the Peace Arch, on the U.S.-Canadian border north of Seattle. This monument was a little more clever given that next to it, on the Canadian side, Sam built a large resort full of liquor for Americans looking to take a vacation from Prohibition.

As Sam got older, he found himself becoming more sentimental for his estranged wife and family. To try and attract them west, he built for them a massive concrete mansion, which he named Maryhill in honor of his wife and daughter. Unfortunately, this mansion was built on his god forsaken property in Eastern Washington. With his family refusing to come west, Sam was left with a bit of a problem, namely what to do with the concrete edifice hulking over the Columbia River. In the end, on the suggestion of one of his mistresses, Sam turned his house in the middle of nowhere into an art museum in the middle of nowhere, somehow getting Queen Marie of Romania to come out and do the dedication. The rest of Sam's life was mostly schemes involving motion pictures and underwater mining, and having elaborate globes made to give away as presents. When he finally died he had himself interred in a monument of his own design near his Stonehenge. A few years after his death the monument crumbled and fell into the Columbia River.

#15 Joshua Norton The First Emperor of The United States

San Francisco in the mid-nineteenth century was a tough place to live, but for the fortunate, there were mountains of money to be made. For many, these mountains were lost just as quickly.

Norton showed up in San Francisco at age of 31 on a boat from South Africa with a million dollar inheritance in his pockets. Norton had a lot of success in Frisco for his first ten years, amassing a considerable fortune of nearly seven million dollars through real estate ventures. It was at this time, hearing of a famine in China, Norton tried to corner the rice market, a venture that fell apart when the price of rice plummeted. Norton, like any good businessman, tried to wiggle his way out of his obligations via the court system. Unfortunately, this ploy failed after years of litigation. Norton's assets were seized and he suddenly found himself in the literal poor house. The whole experience left a decidedly bitter taste in his mouth. With few options available to him, Norton went with the most insane one possible and declared himself Norton I, Emperor of the United States and the Protector of Mexico.

Luckily for Norton, this was a time before even radio, and the people of San Francisco were constantly bored out of their minds. For the local newspapers, which were already reporting on the weekly adventures of two stray dogs, a crazy man publicly declaring himself emperor was a god send. Norton kicked off his reign with a series of edicts aimed at dissolving Congress and arresting every member of the U.S. legislative branch. Congress, in a rather ballsy move, ignored the edict, but the citizens of San Francisco became enamored with their new king, buying him a beautiful blue uniform with golden epaulets, which for you more uncouth readers are the dangly things on the shoulders. Norton further expanded his royal wardrobe with an umbrella, peacock feather and top hat, and a large rosette (those ribbons they hand out at the County Fair). Thus, regally bedecked, Norton would wander the streets, inspecting public buildings and the appearance of police officers, and giving long philosophical speeches to anyone who would listen.

For 21 years Norton ruled over the United States. While most of his edicts were ignored, even the ones that made good sense; such as building a bridge to Oakland or banishing all stray cats; his citizens always treated him with the utmost respect. Though penniless, Norton was allowed to dine at the finest restaurants and was always given a private box at the opening night of every play and show. Norton returned these kindnesses by handing out Imperial Seals of Approval and bestowing titles of nobility. To pay for his debts, Norton issued his own money, which of course had his picture on it, and sold Imperial bonds to tourists. However, Norton's reign was not always easy. He was once arrested by a policeman who, for some reason, thought Norton was insane. Norton was soon after released with an official apology, and being a magnanimous ruler, pardoned the arresting officer. After that, all police officers saluted Norton when he walked by.

San Francisco being full of crazy people, Norton did have one rival in the personage of a phrenologist named George Washington Number Two, a man who was convinced that he was the reincarnation of the first president. GW #2 believed himself to be quite the ladies' man, which mostly involved him showing his bare legs to passersby. He became a thorn in Norton's side for quite some time. When not engaged in his rivalry, Norton spent most of his days writing letters to other world monarchs, many of whom wrote back with amazingly similar handwriting. This culminated in Queen Victoria accepting his offer of marriage. Unfortunately, the royal wedding never took place due to Norton dying. The Emperor's funeral was one of the largest in San Francisco history.

#16 Pocahontas
Can You Paint with All the Colors of the Bullshit?

Pokey was the daughter of Powhatan, the head chief of the Algonquian tribes of Virginia. As was tradition, each tribe sent a woman to Powhatan to bear him a child, at which point they were then sent back to find a new husband. Pokey was one of these children. Pokey's name was said to mean wanton, which can mean either that she enjoyed to play and frolic, or that she was sexually immodest. When Pokey was around 11, a sizable group of English settlers showed up in Virginia and built a town in a swamp. The English called their new settlement Jamestown. Their leader, a self-centered adventurer named John Smith, visited Powhatan to establish relations. Smith, who was a bit of a pathological liar, later claimed that Powhatan tried to crush his head with a club, but that Pokey stopped him. In truth, the two men probably just talked, but that wouldn't have made for a good story.

Following the initial meeting, Pokey often went to Jamestown to visit Smith and to play games with the boys there. Take that sentence however you want. Noticing that the people of Jamestown were starving to death, because they were idiots, she started bringing them food. This lasted for two years until Smith had to go back to England after becoming severely wounded by a gun powder accident. The remaining English, apparently just because they were assholes, told Pokey that Smith had died. After that Pokey quit coming around to play and things between the English and the natives quickly deteriorated into a war which lasted four years. Early in the war, the English captured Pokey and tried to use her as leverage for negotiations with her father to get him to return some stolen guns and tools. Powhatan, having many daughters, did not return all of the items demanded, which resulted in a year long standoff.

During the standoff it was said that Pokey received "extraordinary courteous usage". Again, take that as you will. Whatever was going on, Pokey was also baptized a Christian and renamed Rebecca, because even in time of war, the English couldn't get past the need to save what they considered wayward souls. The standoff built up to a violent confrontation between the two sides, but Pokey, in proper angry daughter fashion, stepped between the two armies and publicly berated her father for not giving up a few guns for her. Then, in a move born of some kind of mix of Stockholm Syndrome and teenage rebelliousness, she married an Englishman named John Rolfe, who was famous for being the first white man to successfully cultivate tobacco. The two sides, now awkward in-laws, made peace. John and Pokey's marriage was a strange one, not because she was 18 and he was 29, but because he considered her a heathen savage, which is probably not the best start to a marriage.

Pokey lived for two years at Jamestown with her new husband, during which time she gave birth to a son. After two years of wedded bliss, Rolfe took her back to England with him to act as a walking tourist attraction and billboard for setting up more colonies in Virginia. Pokey was a big hit in England, attending all of the finest parties and even getting to meet the king. She also got to see her old friend John Smith, which was surprising given that she thought he had been dead for the past eight years. After a year in England, the couple set out for home, but before the ship even got out of the River Thames, Pokey fell ill with smallpox and died. She was 21 years old. Soon after, the Algonquian tribes and English settlers went back to killing each other in Virginia.

#17 Edmund Creffield
Holy Roller Extraordinaire

At the start of the twentieth century a man in his mid-thirties named Edmund became disenchanted with the Salvation Army, because in his words they weren't religious enough. This is somewhat of an interesting statement given that the Salvation Army of the time was much more into beating drums and yelling about hell than it is today. Thoroughly disgusted by their half assery, Edmund decided it would just be best if he started his own religion. Setting up shop in Corvallis, Oregon, Edmund began preaching his new brand of Christianity, called the Brides of Christ, which quickly attracted members of many prominent families around town. The Brides of Christ weren't one of those quiet and demure sects. No, members spent hours screaming and rolling around on the ground, wearing nothing but what amounted to thin white bathrobes, working themselves into a delirious frenzy. For some strange reason, Edmund's new church was comprised mostly well to do women, which probably had nothing to do with the fact that it gave them the perfect opportunity to do something else with their lives besides household chores and catering to the every whim of the men in their lives.

As is to be expected, things got weird fast. First Edmund ordered his congregation to cut themselves off from unbelievers, causing many wives, mothers, and daughters to separate themselves from their families. Then he ordered them to burn all of their worldly possessions, which in the ensuing bonfire apparently included a couple of cats and dogs. This was followed by the entire congregation barricading itself in a house for months, screaming, rolling around on the floor, and doing god knows what else. The men of Corvallis, upset by this chain of events, tarred and feathered Edmund and ran him out of town. However, he soon after returned, now legally married to a woman named Maude, one of his parishioners. By this time, tales of Edmund sleeping with more than just his new wife started to circulate, and a warrant was issued for his arrest for adultery, which back then could land you in jail. After a statewide manhunt, which ended with a dirty Edmund found living under a porch, the holy man was sent to jail for two years. Most of his followers were put in insane asylums, because only a crazy woman would join a sex cult rather than spend her days cleaning house and cooking meals.

When Edmund got out of prison, he re-gathered his flock, most of whom had since been freed from the asylum, and told them that he was the new Jesus and that god would punish the world for imprisoning him. As luck would have it, the San Francisco earthquake happened a few days later. Edmund then told his flock that he needed to sleep with all of them in a purification ritual to prepare one to the be the new Mary, which is confusing given that he thought he was Jesus. However, having seen Edmund destroy San Francisco, his followers just kind of went with it. Edmund then led his cult in an exodus from Corvallis to the Oregon Coast. It was at this point that things began to get ugly. One of the angry husbands tracked the Brides of Christ to the coast and tried to shoot Edmund with a revolver. The revolver didn't go off, increasing Edmund's stature. However, not quite having the same faith in himself as his followers, Edmund then chose to escape to Seattle, taking only his wife Maude and Esther, the woman he had chosen to be the new Mary, with him. The rest of the women were left to starve and freeze on the beach.

Edmund's luck ran out in Seattle. Esther's angry brother, George, tracked the trio down and shot Edmund in the head in broad daylight, killing him instantly. George was arrested, but was later acquitted based on the ruling that it should be okay to shoot someone if they fuck every woman in your family and aren't actually Jesus. Laws were different back then. However, George did not get to enjoy his freedom for long. His sister Esther, a little angry about not getting to be the new Mary, shot him in the head in broad daylight. An unrepentant Esther was declared legally insane, along with Maude for good measure, and the two women were sent to the asylum. Both women later killed themselves. The rest of the flock, somewhat embarrassed, returned home to pretend that none of it had ever happened, spending their days cleaning house and cooking meals.

#18 Pearl Hart
Gangsta As Shit

Technically Pearl was born in Canada, but why let that little technicality get in the way of a good story? At the age of 16, Pearl, a well educated and comely young woman, fell in love with a drunken gambler named Frank Hart and married him in secret. Amazingly enough things did not turn out well given that the only thing Frank enjoyed more than gambling was beating his new wife. Pearl left Frank for a time, but being stupid, as one often is at 16, she soon after went back to him. This cycle perpetuated itself repeatedly for the next six years, during which time, Pearl had two children, both of which were sent to live with her mother. Frank, being a violent alcoholic, often had trouble finding work, so the duo spent a lot of time on the road. Things changed in 1893 when the couple went to the Chicago World's Fair, where Frank got a job as a midway barker. Pearl went to Buffalo Bill's Wild West Show, became enamored with cowboys, and ran away with a piano player, appropriately named Dan Bandman.

Pearl and her new beau took a train to Colorado and then slowly worked their way south to Arizona. This being the time before radios, it was not hard for a good piano player to find work. Unfortunately, Bandman was not what one would consider a good piano player. Pearl ended up trying to supplement their income, first by singing accompaniment to Bandman's patent abuse of the ivories, which did little to improve the overall quality of the music, then second by working as a cook, which might have worked out better if she actually knew how to cook. Broke and desperate, Bandman, an entrepreneur, used the only asset he had on hand to make a living, Pearl's 22 year old body. While some might call this prostitution, Bandman preferred to call Pearl a demimondaine, which is a fancy French term for prostitute. This less than equitable arrangement went on for five years, during which for some reason Pearl developed a fondness for cigars, liquor, and morphine. In 1898, Bandman left to fight in the Spanish-American War. Pearl told him she hoped the Spanish killed him. With no other skills to make a living, Pearl set up a tent brothel outside a local mine, which went okay until the mine closed.

In need of money, Pearl convinced one of her former customers, Joe Boot, to help her rob a stagecoach, an interesting move given that this was 1899, but let's face it, none of Pearl's other decisions had been that great. The robbery, which took place in the Arizona desert and involved Pearl dressed in men's clothing, was a great success, netting the pair what amounted to $12,000 in today's money. Unfortunately, Pearl and Joe then got lost in the desert and were arrested not long after. The news of a female stagecoach robber sparked a media frenzy and Pearl soon found herself a celebrity, conducting numerous interviews for local and national newspapers. While Joe sat in a prison cell, Pearl was just locked in a normal room and even got to keep a bobcat cub as a pet. Taking advantage of her captors' sexist underestimation, Pearl escaped by simply kicking a hole in the wall, but was recaptured two weeks later. During the trial, Pearl claimed she was only trying to raise money to get back to her sick mother. The jury soon after declared her innocent. A little pissed off at this turn of events, the authorities brought new charges of mail tampering against her, which the jury apparently took more seriously. Pearl declared she would recognize no law that treated her like a second hand citizen. The jury declared her guilty and sentenced her to five years in prison. Joe got thirty.

Pearl served her sentence in Yuma, where she was the only woman in the prison, a fact she used to her advantage by trading certain favors with the guards and warden to improve her situation. Pearl enjoyed an oversized cell with a good view and its own yard. She was also allowed to entertain reporters and other guests and pose for photographs. Even with all of these amenities Pearl did not enjoy prison. She first tried to get early release by claiming she was needed to star in a play in Kansas City about her life. When that didn't work, she changed her tune and claimed she was pregnant. Wishing to avoid a scandal the governor pardoned Pearl in 1902 and provided her with a train ticket to Kansas City. Pearl's life after her release faded into the unknown. She did star in a short lived play about her life, using the proceeds to purchase a cigar store. After that she just kind of disappeared, though many claim she lived into the 1950's.

#19 Matthew Hensen
The Ice Man Cometh

In 1909 explorer Robert Peary, using nothing but his amazing mustache, became the first man to reach the North Pole, earning him numerous accolades and a permanent place in the history books. Of course, it was all bullshit. The one that should've been talked about was Matt.

Matt did not have good luck when it came to family. Born to a family of sharecroppers at the end of the Civil War his mother died when he was two. His father, seeking better opportunities, moved the family to Washington DC. However, instead of finding opportunities, Matt's father also died. Matt was then passed on to an uncle who paid for him to get some education, but of course the uncle soon died as well. Out of living family members, Matt worked as a dishwasher until he was 11, at which point he decided dish washing was bullshit, walked his ass to Baltimore, and became a cabin boy on an ocean freighter. The captain of the ship took a shine to young Matt, and took it upon himself to further educate him as they traveled around the world for the next seven years, at which point the captain died and Matt found himself out of work again.

Back in Washington DC, Matt found himself work at a hat shop. It was at this point that he met Peary who, ordered to lead an expedition to Nicaragua to map a possible route for a canal, was in the market for a sun hat. Peary, impressed with Matt's seamanship, offered him a job. Matt, not really into the whole hat selling gig, accepted. Peary found Matt to be most helpful in Nicaragua, leading him to look for the young man again in 1892 when he was planning an expedition to Greenland. Peary offered Matt a place as his right hand man. Matt, now a married man, apparently couldn't recognize Peary as a certifiable crazy person, and accepted without consulting his wife. The two men left soon after for Greenland, but the expedition hit a bit of a snag when Peary broke his leg only a few days after arriving. While Peary recuperated, Matt did some exploring, made friends with the Inuit, and learned their language. Peary mostly sat on his ass and wrote wild claims of his discoveries in his journal. After two years in the Arctic, Matt returned home to find an understandably upset wife who wanted a divorce.

The two men returned to Greenland in 1896 and 1898 where, thanks to Matt's work with the Inuit, they perfected their Arctic survival skills by basically doing whatever the Inuit did, an idea that had not been considered by previous explorers. Peary, never one to worry about who deserves credit for what, called the techniques they developed the Peary System. The Peary System mostly involved having Matt and their Inuit guides do all the work, laying supply caches for later use, and eating sled dogs. With the "Peary System" perfected, Peary decided it was time to start pushing for the North Pole. Despite funding from the U.S. government, which for some reason thought reaching the North Pole was a good use of tax dollars, expeditions in 1902 and 1905 both failed. It was at this time that Peary and Matt, despite Peary being married and both being in their forties, married Inuit women, by which I mean fourteen year old girls, who pumped out a couple of children, which the two men then subsequently abandoned when they went home.

In 1909, Matt and Peary, in their final expedition, managed to reach the North Pole. The prior sentence should actually read Matt and four Inuit guides managed to reach the North Pole, because at that point Peary had lost eight of his toes to frost bite and was unable to walk, making him pretty much luggage in the sled, something that he seemingly forgot to include in his journal. It being the very racist early twentieth century, Peary returned home to a hero's welcome, while Matt was rewarded with a nice dinner at a so-so restaurant. The four Inuit guides meanwhile went back to their lives of desperately trying not to freeze to death. Peary lived out the remainder of his life living on a generous government pension and defending himself against claims he had lied and never actually reached the North Pole. Matt lived out the remainder of his life working a low level position at a Customs House until he died at the age of 89.

#20 Lizzie Borden
Forty Whacks

In 1892, Andrew and Abby Borden were murdered by a psychopath with a hatchet. Andrew was a fairly well to do man, worth $8 million in today's cash. However, that didn't keep him from living his life rather frugally, living in a modes two story house, with no indoor plumbing, in a fairly average neighborhood. Abby was Andrew's second wife, and with them lived Andrew's two spinster daughters from his first marriage, Emma age 41 and Lizzie age 32, plus a live in maid. The Borden household was not a happy one. Both Emma and Lizzie were convinced that Abby was a gold digging bitch who was just after their father's money, and Abby thought the two girls should go out and find husbands, or at the very least, do something besides sit around and wait for their father to die. Of the two daughters, Lizzie was the most incensed over the whole thing, especially when Andrew started giving property to Abby's relatives, and then gave Abby some of this first wife's jewelry. But perhaps what really threw her over the edge was when Andrew killed all the pigeons in the barn with a hatchet, pigeons Lizzie had been treating as pets.

The investigation was of course fucked up from the get go. Lizzie claimed to have discovered the bodies, but upon the police arriving she changed her story several times until settling on she had been in the hayloft in the barn for over half an hour, despite the stifling heat, either searching for fishing line weights or eating pears. The police did a cursory search of the house, uncovering a freshly cleaned hatchet with a broken off handle, but decided it probably wasn't that important. They then, in an act of stupid gallantry, agreed to come back later since Lizzie was feeling unwell, leaving all of the evidence at the house. The overly chivalrous police returned two days later to find a suspiciously calm and well poised Lizzie ready to answer all of their questions. They also found a bucket of bloody rags in the basement, which none of them would get near because Lizzie claimed they were menstrual rags (tampons having not been invented yet), and a half burned dress in the stove, which Lizzie claimed she had burned because it got paint on it, as one does. The police, seeing nothing weird about any of this, went back on their merry way. Who knows what finally convinced them Lizzie might be a suspect, perhaps it was the local druggist telling them that Lizzie had tried to buy poison a few days before the murder, but they finally arrested her a week after the deed was done.

The trial was one of the first sensational trials of the century, watched by the entire nation, which is unfortunate given it made Massachusetts look like a state full of idiots. The judge, a stickler for obtuse rules, refused to let half of the evidence be seen; the police, under oath, admitted they were bungling idiots; and the prosecutor, aside from being a plain old nut, was a man prone to fits of rage and grandiose gestures. It probably didn't help any that the judge had been appointed to his position by one of Lizzie's attorneys, who had formerly been the governor. It definitely didn't help that the prosecutor thought it would a good idea to display Andrew and Abby's severed heads (the actual heads, not photographs), as evidence. Lizzie fainting did little to help his case. The jury, long on fancy mustaches and beards, but short on common sense, declared Lizzie not guilty after only 90 minutes of deliberation.

Most people acquitted of murder would leave town afterwards, especially if everyone in town thought they did it. Not Lizzie. She took her father's millions and bought a big house in the nicest part of town and then started throwing parties attended by famous actresses. She also changed her named to Lizbeth, because when you're rich you can call yourself whatever the hell you want. The case to this day remains officially unsolved, though theories abound. The two best ones are that the maid did it, because Andrew forced her to wash windows when she was feeling unwell, and that Lizzie did it because she was caught in a lesbian tryst with the maid. This last one seems somewhat doubtful given that Lizzie, unable to remember the maid's name, just called her Maggie (her name was Brigid). The Borden house is now a murder themed bed and breakfast, so I guess there's that.

#21 Hetty Green
The Witch of Wall Street

Ebenezer Scrooge was real, just not with the genitals you expected. Hetty Green was the richest woman alive in the late nineteenth century, worth over $4 billion in today's money (it will all be in today's money). Hetty made her money through shrewd conservative investing, staying calm when others panicked, and being cheap as hell.

Hetty was born into a wealthy whaling family to a workaholic father and a sickly mother. She spent most of her childhood at her father's side, learning the ins and outs of business. The woman could barely write a legible sentence, but by age 6 she was reading stock quotes every evening. Hetty's father tried to marry her off when she came of age, giving her a new wardrobe worth thousands of dollars. Hetty sold the clothes and invested in the stock market. Her father died shortly after the end of the Civil War, leaving her a sizable fortune of $77 million. Hetty celebrated by marrying Edward Green, a man of enough means that he'd keep his hands off her money. She then celebrated her nuptials by forging her recently deceased Aunt Sylvia's will in an attempt to score another $30 million that had been willed to charity. This did not work out well and Hetty was forced to flee to London to escape forgery charges.

In London, Hetty gave birth to two children, Ned and Sylvia (because if you're going to try to defraud your dead aunt you might as well name your kid after them), and started making money hand over fist by buying paper U.S. dollars that were issued during the Civil War. Once the statute of limitations was up, Hetty and Edward moved their family back to New York, where Hetty started investing in railroads, speculating on the stock market, and buying up mortgages. As her fortune grew, she also started lending money to bankers and brokerage houses. Everything she touched turned to gold. However, when it came to light that Edward had been using some of her money, Hetty took the children and left. It was at this point that things began to go off the rails.

Not seeing much reason to be a spendthrift, Hetty moved her family into a tiny apartment with no heat or hot water (partly to try to hide from the taxman). When her children complained of the cold, she stuffed their clothes with old newspapers. When Ned hurt his leg, Hetty tried to take him to the local free clinic, but was forced to flee when she was recognized as one of the richest women in the country. Refusing to pay for a doctor she instead let Ned's leg get infected to the point where it had to be amputated, which she forced her estranged husband to pay for. As Hetty got older she became even more miserly. At the same time that Hetty was making several multi-million dollar loans to New York City and some of the largest banks in the country to help keep them solvent, she was wearing the same black dress that she had worn every day for years on end. It's probably also worth mentioning that she commanded her laundress to only wash the dirty parts of the dress in order to save on soap.

Hetty's frugality became the stuff of legends. For twenty years she suffered from a painful hernia, which she held in by jamming a small stick in her underwear. When it became too much a problem she went to a doctor who promptly told her he could fix it for $3,500. In response, Hetty calmly put the stick back in her underwear and left. Hetty worked each day in a cold dark office, subsisting off dry oatmeal she heated on another office's radiator. Though she kept half a billion in cash on hand at all times she lived off of $200 a week. Once she lost a 2 cent stamp in her carriage and spent the entire night looking for it. The only thing she spent money on was her beloved dog Curtis, whose name she put on her front door to confuse the taxman. Paranoid of kidnappers, she slept with a revolver tied to her wrist with a string. After Hetty died her vast fortune went to Ned and Sylvia. Sylvia built herself a mansion and mostly kept to herself. Ned gave himself the nickname Colonel, married a hooker named Mabel, and threw lavish and extravagant parties. When Ned died his share went to his sister. When Sylvia died she gave a final fuck you to her mother by donating the $90 million of the fortune that remained to charity.

#22 Edwin Forrest
Actors Have Always Been Crazy

In the mid-nineteenth century Eddie was the most famous Shakespearean actor in all of the United States, but he wanted more; he wanted to be the most famous in the world.

Young Eddie, the son of a banker, was no different than most 14 year olds at the time, in that he had no idea what the hell he wanted to do. Jumping from apprenticeship to apprenticeship, nothing seemed like a good fit. Eddie was discovered the same way most actors today are, at a drug party. Eddie, high out of his gourd on nitrous oxide, the drug of choice for the affluent back then, launched into a soliloquy that so impressed some local thespians that they asked if he had ever acted before. When he told them that as a child he had played a girl in a melodrama, they gave him an audition on the spot. Eddie started his career acting in theaters across the southern and western U.S., the equivalent of doing commercials and B-movies today. During this time, he gained fame for his blackface caricature, which was said to be so good that it fooled African Americans, though to be fair, this was a time when slavery was still legal, so it wasn't like they could just tell him to fuck off. Eddie's big break came at age 23 when he started playing Shakespeare parts in New York City and Philadelphia, gaining widespread fame and accolades.

Having achieved fame in America, Eddie traveled to London where he garnered further acclaim. It was here that Eddie met William Macready, the most famous Shakespearean actor in all of England. The two got along well as friendly rivals. Eddie soon after returned to America so pleased with his trip that he married an English woman. Nine years later, now a man of 39, Eddie returned to England. Things did not go well a second time. The theatergoers in London did not like his take on Macbeth and hissed at him. Eddie took offense and, for god only knows what reason, blamed the hissing on the jealous machinations of Willy. Seeking revenge, Eddie traveled to Edinburgh, where Willy was playing Hamlet, rented a private box, and hissed at him. This act insulted the Englishman's fragile pride, leading him to call Eddie, "without taste", which is an old timey way of saying he was a piece of shit. Eddie was forced to return to the U.S. as a reviled man.

The next four years were rough on Eddie. Pretty sick of England, he soon after separated from his wife due to becoming suspicious that she might be cheating on him, a thought that probably entered his head because he was cheating on her. Even worse, his rival Willy came to America to tour and prove once and for all who was the better actor. Incensed, Eddie stalked Willy across the country, appearing in the same plays just days after Willy left. Over time their rivalry began to represent the class warfare of the day, with Eddie representing the working class stiffs and Willy representing the gentile aristocracy, because nothing sounds more aristocratic than a fancy accent. The rich guffawed and dropped their monocles in shock at Eddie's antics. The poor threw half a dead sheep onto the stage at Willy's feet. Things finally came to a head when both men played Macbeth in New York City at two theaters very close to each other. Eddie's fans, being the classiest, threw eggs and garbage at Willy on opening night and hissed and booed so loudly that no one was able to hear the play. Three nights later Willy again took the stage. This time Eddie's fans started a riot and tried to burn down the theater. While Willy escaped in disguise, the city called out the state militia which started randomly shooting people, killing 30and injuring 210. This in turn led to a second riot the next day.

Disgusted at it all, Willy returned to England and soon after happily retired. Eddie became involved in an overly dramatic and heavily reported upon divorce. Highlights included Eddie beating his wife's alleged lover with a whip and his wife claiming that what Eddie thought was cheating as actually being just amateur phrenology. The whole experience left Eddie decidedly sour. However, he stayed in the theater for years afterward, continuing to have success until he developed severe gout at age 59, causing him to suffer from an unsteady gait and lose the use of one of his hands. His career went downhill from there, after which he spent most of his time in his castle like mansion on the Hudson River, leading several philanthropic efforts and thinking up ways to avoid paying alimony owed to his ex-wife. He died of a stroke at the age of 66, which probably had nothing to do with him being a little high strung.

#23 Parker French
A Man of Confidence

The world is full of people of genius. Many of these people go on to do great things. Parker used his genius to spend his life scamming people.

Parker was born in Kentucky in the early 1820's and soon became an orphan for reasons that are not important to this story. Raised by a kindly local judge, Parker received the best education possible until he got bored, ran away, and joined the British Navy. Several years later he returned, his pockets stuffed with cash, and thanked the judge for his past kindness by marrying the man's daughter. Everything started to go to shit from there. Parker's first scam was to collect money to build a ship to take people to the Californian gold mines. The fact that Parker lived in St. Louis, which is decidedly not near the ocean, should have been a tip off that things weren't on the up and up, but people were more trusting back then. When the scam was found out, Parker skedaddled to New York City and, just to show that he had a sense of humor about the whole thing, granted himself the title of Captain.

In New York City, Parker started signing up people again for an expedition to California, promising to get them there within sixty days. Numerous people, greedy for gold, paid to join up and Parker used their money to live an exorbitant lifestyle. After several months of delays Parker got his shit together enough to get the expedition out of New York, sailing to Texas, which as some of you have probably noticed, is not California. Never a man to back down from a challenge, Parker told the expedition that it would be quicker to head overland across the arid Southwest. To accomplish this feat, he purchased some old circus wagons and several tons of food using fraudulent letters of credit from some of the biggest shipping firms in New York. However, all good things come to an end. Parker's creditors caught up to his decidedly colorful wagon train by the time he reached El Paso. Not ready to face the music, Parker fled with a couple of cohorts into Mexico, abandoning the expedition members to find their own damn way home. A small group of these cheated potential gold miners, pissed off for some reason, tried to hunt Parker down, but he and his thugs ambushed them. During the resulting gunfight Parker was shot in the arm, leading to it getting amputated.

Parker stayed in Mexico for a time, running several cons and robbing ranchers at gunpoint. Finally tiring of his shit, Mexico locked him in jail, but released him eighteen months later when he promised to get the hell out of the country. Parker made his way north to California where he set himself up as a newspaper man, a job which made him popular enough that he managed to get himself elected to the state legislature. To celebrate, he punched a former governor in the face and got shot in the leg. Finding politics rather boring, Parker abandoned his post in 1855 to join William Walker's invasion of Nicaragua, granting himself the title of Colonel because why hell not. When the invasion succeeded, Walker declared Parker the new government's ambassador to the United States. The U.S. government, less than impressed with the whole thing, refused to meet with Parker, so he instead held lavish parties and went on a speaking tour to raise funds and recruit more soldiers. However, as always, most of the cash he raised ended up in his own pocket. Parker then tried to return to Nicaragua, but by then Walker was rather tired of his shit and wouldn't let him stay.

Things began to unravel after that. Over the next fifteen years Parker and his wife crisscrossed the country, running various scams to arrive. These scams included a land scheme in Minnesota, a fake newspaper in San Francisco, an imaginary opium shipment in New Orleans, something involving ginseng, and the selling of non-existent ships to the U.S. Navy in Boston. During the Civil War he was imprisoned for a time on the suspicion he might be a Confederate spy, but even that turned out to be only part of some elaborate scam. After getting set free, he did a few more scams just to keep a roof over his head and then disappeared from history. His last known whereabouts was living in a gutter in Washington D.C., slowly killing himself with cocktails of whiskey and chloroform.

#24 Carrie Nation
A Blitzkrieg on Booze

Carrie was a tank of a woman. Standing at 6 feet tall and weighing in at 175 pounds, she described herself as a bulldog, running along at the feet of Jesus, barking at what he didn't like.

Carrie was born under some pretty piss poor conditions. Her father was a hard luck man who failed at every business he tried, and her mother was a woman who loved finery and social airs, but suffered from delusions that often times left her convinced that she was Queen Victoria. Due to these two familial quirks, the family moved constantly throughout Carrie's childhood, leaving little time for formal education. What little schooling Carrie did get came from random books she managed to get her hands on and the family bible. After the Civil War, Carrie fell in love with a young physician named Charles Gloyd, who, as luck would have it, happened to be a severe alcoholic. Carrie's parents did not like the match, what with Gloyd being a drunk and all, but Carrie was smitten. Gloyd unsurprisingly died a little over a year later, his liver pickled the maximum amount possible. Carrie, unfazed, used his estate to build herself a nice little home and get her teaching license.

At age 28, Carrie got remarried to a minister and attorney 19 years her senior named David Nation. The couple lived in Texas for a time until David got involved in local politics, by which I mean several of the local politicians murdered each other. Not holding his beliefs that tightly, David and Carrie then moved to Kansas where David made a pittance working as a minister and Carrie made good money running a hotel. However, the hotel apparently didn't take up enough of Carrie's time for she soon founded a local temperance movement. At the time, due to the prevalence of drunken cowboys, Kansas had banned the sale of booze, but the law wasn't really being enforced and saloons operated openly. Carrie, a woman of action, spent her time off going to bars and singing hymns to the drunks, which unsurprisingly had little effect.

After nine frustrating years of hymn singing, Carrie, now a woman of 54, had a bit of a revelation, or perhaps a breakdown. Convinced that God had given her a divine order in a dream, she collected a big pile of rocks, took them to a saloon, and smashed all the liquor bottles. After destroying two more saloons in a similar fashion a tornado struck Kansas, which Carrie took to be a thumbs up from the man upstairs. More raids followed, after which her husband David sarcastically suggested that a hatchet would be more effective. Carrie, believing it to be the first sensible advice the man had ever given her, divorced her husband and then bought herself a hatchet. With her new weapon in hand, Carrie began a reign of terror across the country, smashing taverns wherever she found them. She was arrested and fined numerous times, but was unapologetic. The fines were paid off using money she earned doing speaking engagements, autographing pictures of herself, and selling souvenir hatchets to her many admirers.

Carrie Nation became big business to the point where she trademarked her own name. When President McKinley was shot, Carrie, believing him to be a secret drunk, applauded the act because drinkers get what they deserve. As her fame grew a vaudeville group, for god only knows what reason, convinced her to join them on a tour to England. Carrie, evidently not understanding what vaudeville was, spent her time on stage giving sermons on the evil of drink, which were rebutted with eggs thrown by the audience. It didn't take long for Carrie to understand that she was being treated as some type of joke, so she ripped up her contract and went back to the American speaking circuit. In the middle of one of these lectures she collapsed on stage and died at the age of 64.

#25 Hillary Clinton
That's Ms. Rodham If Your Nasty

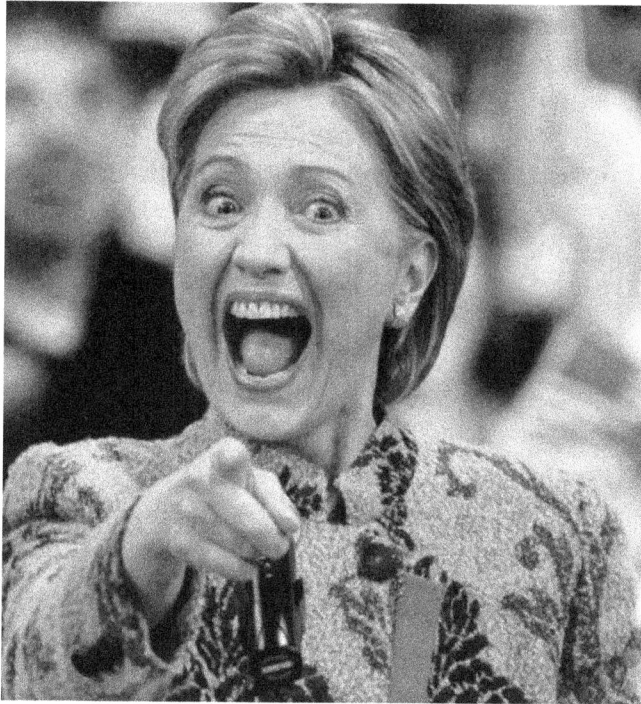

Pantsuit was born in to a fairly boring middle-class family. When she was a little girl she wrote a letter to NASA saying she wanted to be an astronaut. NASA, apparently not having enough to do sending people to the moon, replied with a letter saying a female astronaut was a stupid idea. Somewhat upset by this, Pantsuit swore she would do everything in her power to prove that a woman could do anything that a man could do. Her first step in this epic quest was attending an all women's college. Her second step was to hook herself up with a womanizer nicknamed Bubba, staying an extra year at school just to be with him. As far as plans went, it didn't really make a whole lot of sense. Despite such setbacks, Pantsuit rallied on, gaining accolades, earning respect, and sparking predictions of a tremendous future law career. With such high hopes she of course failed the bar exam her first try, which she dealt with by marrying Bubba and agreeing to support him in his political career. Again, not exactly the best laid out plan.

For a time, Pantsuit tried to be an independent woman, working as a lawyer and keeping her own last name, but over time the weight of voter expectations (voters mostly being yokels in this case), wore her down until she morphed into the demure woman the American voter demanded. Bubba got elected president and Pantsuit learned to be a political chameleon, appearing as whatever people wanted her to be, until nobody, including herself, was really sure what she was. This made Pantsuit a very secretive person, paranoid to the point where she wouldn't even let anyone read her college thesis. She also got in the habit of countering anyone calling her a liar by calling them a liar, a tactic that worked amazingly well. Pantsuit spent a good chunk of Bubba's presidency claiming his many affairs were part of some kind of vast conspiracy against the two of them and plotting on how she could become president. Pantsuit wanted to prove to the world that a woman could president. Which was a very different goal than her husband's, who mostly seemed to become president for just the hot chubby intern action. Pantsuit began her march to the presidency by becoming a senator for New York, a state in which she had never lived. She then ran for the presidency in 2008, but was beaten by a man whose spouse had never sexually harassed anyone. Pantsuit became Secretary of State, and waited around for her chance to run again eight years later.

In 2016, Pantsuit was sure she was going to be elected president. We're talking so sure that she probably already bought monogrammed towels. To be fair, she was a poised well informed candidate running against a shaved misogynistic racist baboon who openly talked about groping women. How could she lose? Well, apparently she could, because she did. Some say she lost because over the previous eight years a significant part of the country suddenly became racist and misogynistic again. Some claim it was because she couldn't connect with younger voters. Perhaps it was the fact that her every smile seemed kind of fake and her every reaction a calculated veneer. Maybe it was because, like your grandmother, she had absolutely zero knowledge of how technology works (seriously, the woman doesn't even know how to run a desktop). It most definitely didn't help that when a scandal broke out about her using private emails for official business, she decided that it would be a better option to have some people believe she was a Machiavellian genius rather than an out of touch luddite.

In the end, the election was decided the same as so many others, by a group of probably drunk laid off factory workers from the Rust Belt, who upon realizing that neither party really gives a shit about them, vote for whichever candidate seems like the biggest middle finger to the current establishment. Whatever the reason, Pantsuit hid herself away, wrote a concession speech she never thought she'd have to give, and now has to move on with her life. What is she going to do? Who knows, but hopefully it involves buying herself one of those Computers for Dumbasses books.

#26 Jack Parsons
Rocket Man

Jack grew up in a broken home (his father was a depressed adulterer) and spent most of his childhood reading alone and blowing shit up. Jack loved explosives. His extremely patient mother put up with his hobby, but was horrified when she caught him trying to do a supposed occult ritual to summon the devil. Jack was sent to military school to straighten him out, but it wasn't long before he was expelled for blowing up toilets. Exasperated, his mother then sent him to a very liberal private school that didn't give grades and let its students do whatever the hell they wanted. What Jack wanted to do was blow shit up, work for explosives manufacturers, and write letters to famous rocket scientists, all of which he did. Though too poor to attend college, Jack started hanging out with several CalTech science students, bribing them with marijuana in order to gain access to the science labs. Together, Jack and his new friends formed a rocketry club, which also wrote pro-communist science fiction screenplays which they sent to Hollywood, because of course those two things go together.

As the country suffered through the Great Depression, Jack and his club built rockets out in the desert. It was around this time that he married Helen Northrup, a woman he met at a church dance, the place where all pot smoking socialists meet their wives. The marriage was a little rocky, with Jack spending all of their money on rockets (even once pawning her wedding ring) and making homemade nitroglycerin on the front porch. When World War II broke out Jack and his fellow club members, in a convoluted scheme to avoid the draft, founded the Jet Propulsion Laboratory (JPL) and convinced the military to fund their research into rocket powered planes. Over the next several years Jack developed rocket fuels and engines which would later propel humans into space. Being such a genius he of course became inspired to join a cult. The cult of Thelema, founded by Alestair Crowley, who claimed Egyptian gods told him of the dawning of a new age, believed in spiritualism, cosmology, the finding of one's true path, and of course sexual promiscuity. How sexually promiscuous do you ask? Well, when his wife Helen left for a trip, Jack started sleeping with her 17 year old sister Sara. When Helen got back, Sara declared that she was Jack's new wife because she was better at having sexing with him. When Jack agreed, Helen took a new lover and all four moved in together.

Things of course got weird. Jack poured all his money into the cult, buying a compound where they lived as a commune and slaughtered their own animals for food and blood rituals. He started walking around with a large snake draped across his shoulders and sleeping with every woman at the compound and at work, even the married ones. Though to be fair, he always politely paid for any needed abortions. Jack also started using large amounts of peyote, meth, and opiates, because what's the point of running a cult compound if you can't be high as shit the whole time? As the war began to wind down Jack left the JPL and rocketry to focus on the occult. It was around this time that L. Ron Hubbard (later the founder of Scientology) moved into the compound. Jack's main squeeze Sara was quite taken with Hubbard to the point that she started sleeping with him. Jack dealt with this by masturbating on sacred tablets in an attempt to call forth a goddess to have sex with him. Soon after a random vivacious woman named Marjorie Cameron showed up, and lo and behold, she did start having sex with Jack, so maybe don't be so quick to judge. Together, with Hubbard watching, Jack and Marjorie involved themselves in sex magic rituals. At least they did until Hubbard and Sara ran off with all of Jack's money.

Downtrodden, Jack quit the cult, claiming it wasn't culty enough for him, married Marjorie, and moved into a small house where he set aside an area for chemistry experiments and the homebrewing of absinthe. Jack tried to find a job, but had difficulties because he had been black balled by the government. No, not for being part of a drug fueled sex cult, but for writing communist themed screenplays when he was just out of high school. Such was the 1950's. To make ends meet Jack got work making fake fog and imitation bullet wounds for movies. Marjorie left him for a time to join a commune in Mexico, but came back after a few years. Jack made plans to go to Israel to get back into rocketry, but before he could, accidentally blew himself up in the lab he had set up in his home. Marjorie of course then went on to found her own cult called the Moon Children.

#27 Cathay Williams
Penis Required

Cathay did not have an easy life. First her name was Cathay, which was a really old-timey way of saying China, which is kind of weird given that she was not Chinese. Second, she was black in pre-Civil War America, which pretty much most people agree was definitely not the cat's pajamas. Cathay was born to a free black man and an enslaved woman, which according to the laws in Missouri at the time, made her a slave. Cathay spent her childhood working as a house servant, seeing to the needs of the wealthy aristocratic family who owned her. When Cathay was nineteen years old the Civil War broke out, and fearing that Missouri might at any moment break away to join the Confederacy, the Union Army occupied the state. Now the casual observer of history might think that this would be a good thing for Cathay. They would be wrong. The Union Army considered captured slaves contraband, and so instead of slaving away for some rich assholes, Cathay instead was forced to slave away for a bunch of military assholes.

Over the next four years Cathay, though declared a free woman, was forced to do whatever the Union Army told her to do. Luckily for her this was mostly just cooking and laundry. Cathay marched with the army wherever they went, covering a good chunk of the country in doing so. The army couldn't seem to decide whether the slaves they freed were people or property. On one hand they did pay a wage, though a meager one, but on the other they really didn't give people like Cathay much of a choice, often transferring them to other units as though they were enlisted soldiers. This confusion ended with the Civil War. No, the army didn't decide that the former slaves were people, they just decided it wasn't their damn problem to figure it out. Cathay was left free to do whatever the hell she wanted, which unfortunately, without a job, mostly looked like starving to death.

Cathay was not the kind of person to just lay down and quit. Instead she dressed up in man clothes, changed her name to William Cathay, went to an army recruiting office, and joined one of the black only regiments that was being sent to the frontier to fight Native Americans. Being taller than many men of the era (she was five foot nine), the recruiter didn't bat an eye when he signed her up. Things were helped by the fact that the army's medical examination at the time mostly consisted of a drunk doctor giving you a cursory glance to make sure you probably wouldn't die within the next few days. With her unit Cathay traveled westward through Kansas to New Mexico to guard prospectors from the Apache. She didn't have much luck in the army. Cathay was almost immediately hospitalized for small pox and throughout her career would be hospitalized five more times for various ailments. Not one of these times did the doctors discover she was missing a penis, which really speaks to the hands off approach of 1860's medicine.

After two years in the army, mostly performing garrison duty, Cathay got sick again. The doctor, believing in new-fangled medical techniques like actually examining and touching patients, quickly discovered her secret and reported it. Cathay was soon after discharged for her definite lack of a penis, which her commanding officer reported by stating that she had always been both physically and mentally feeble. Cathay spent the next two years working as a cook for the army again, followed by twenty-one years of working as a laundress in Colorado. When her health began to fail to she applied for a military pension. The military sent out an examiner who, despite the fact all of her toes had been amputated and that she needed a crutch to get around, declared her the picture of health. Then, to be a total jerk, he casually added that it didn't matter, since only people with penises were allowed to get military pensions. Cathay died not long after.

#28 Boston Corbett
Enough Balls to Shoot John Wilkes Booth

We've all heard the term "mad hatter", but few men exemplified it quite like Thomas Corbett. Tommy emigrated to the United States from England when he was still a child, and while living in New York, became an apprentice hat maker. Now the hatters of the time used mercury nitrate to turn the fur of beavers and other animals into felt. For the record, excessive exposure to mercury nitrate can lead to hallucinations, psychosis, and twitching (which people called the hatter's shakes). This being the mid-nineteenth century, instead of wondering what might be making all the hatters go insane, people just assumed that it was an industry that attracted eccentric people. Not to say that some people didn't suspect something, but let's face it, changing things meant not having some pretty damn nice hats and nobody wanted that. Tommy worked his whole life as a hatter, only taking a short break to become a homeless drunk in Boston when his wife and baby died in childbirth. One night, after some seriously heavy drinking, a Methodist preacher found Tommy in the gutter and preached at him a while. It must have been some mighty fine preaching because Tommy got religion, never drank again, and changed his name to Boston.

The newly christened Boston got his life back together, going to church every day, and getting a new hatter job to boot. However, he didn't have many friends, probably because he spent all of his time preaching and praying, often stopping work to pray any time one of his co-workers cussed, which given he worked with a bunch of looney hatters, was quite often. Boston also sermonized on street corners, bellowing about the joys of heaven and terrors of hell, earning himself a local reputation as a harmless eccentric. To emulate Jesus, he grew his hair down past his shoulders. Now some might say it would be unfair to call Boston a religious nut, but you can just be the judge of that after these next few sentences. At age twenty-six, after a hard day of street sermonizing, Boston was propositioned by two prostitutes. Deeply disturbed by what most of us would call a boner, but what Boston thought of as a one way ticket to Satan's penthouse, Boston fled to his boardinghouse, read a couple of bible verses, and then castrated himself with a pair of scissors. Feeling holier, he ate a meal, went to church, and then finally went to see a doctor.

When the Civil War started Boston joined the Union Army, because while boners were impure, killing rebels was apparently still A-Okay. Boston did not do well in the army. He read out loud from his bible night and day, held unauthorized prayer meetings, refused to follow orders he thought unholy, and verbally reprimanded his superiors for using foul language. Tiring of this shit, the army court-martialed him and were going to shoot him, but instead decided that a dishonorable discharge was probably the less crazy choice. Boston then re-enlisted with a different army unit, because keeping accurate records hadn't evolved past the "idea" stage back then, and promptly got himself captured and taken to Andersonville prison, a place so terrible that a quarter of the prison population died from shitting themselves to death. As for the survivors, they though the dead were the lucky ones. Boston was freed in a prisoner exchange five months later, after which, instead of being discharged, he was nursed back to health, promoted to sergeant, and sent off with the group responsible for hunting down John Wilkes Booth after he assassinated President Lincoln. The army was ordered to capture Booth alive, so when they found him holed up in a barn they lit it on fire. Boston then heroically shot him through a crack in the wall.

For not following orders, Boston was court martialed again, but then pardoned, because shooting Booth, instead of capturing him, just made things easier. After being discharged from the army, Boston went back to being a hat maker, but was soon fired for his fanatical behavior and paranoia. Convinced people were trying to murder him, he took to randomly pulling his pistol out and waving it around at the most inopportune moments. Boston tried to make money by lecturing on how he killed Booth to Sunday schools and women's groups, but this failed, because nobody likes incoherent speeches and random pistol brandishings. He then worked for the Kansas legislature as a doorman, but after pointing his pistol at several of the legislatures, was sent to an insane asylum. A little over a year later he escaped to Minnesota, where he was presumed killed in the Great Hinckley Fire which consumed 250,000 acres and 420 people.

#29 Ernest Hemingway
Papa Was a Little Nuts

Ernie's life did not have a normal beginning. His mother, not wanting a boy, put him in dresses, only gave him dolls to play with, often called him Ernestine, and told everyone he was his sister's twin (which is weird given she was a year older than him). Ernie's father apparently just went with it, letting things continue as they were for five years. For some strange reason, when Ernie grew up he became super hyper-masculine. To prove just how manly he was, Ernie volunteered to be an ambulance driver in Italy during World War I. This went about as well as could be expected, with him getting wounded and hospitalized for six months, during which time he fell in love with a nurse seven years his senior. The two were supposed to get married, but she changed her mind, calling him a little boy in the process, and leaving him with a healthy dose of relationship anxiety to go along with his gender anxiety. Upon returning to the U.S., Ernie got a journalist job and married a woman eight years his senior named Hadley (who also happened to be his roommate's sister). The couple then moved to Paris.

In Paris, Ernie became a Bohemian, writing short stories and novels (a good chunk of which Hadley lost at a train station), hanging out with the famous artists of the day, going to Spain to watch bullfights, and spending most of his time getting drunk and fighting. Hadley for her part worked several jobs to support Ernie's writing career, and since they were both so busy, they often left their baby son alone in the house to be babysat by their cat. So, you know, all pretty hum-drum stuff. It was during this time that Ernie gained literary success by writing a book about a dickless man and a slutty woman. He then left his wife for a rich hot woman named Paulina (who he was introduced to by his wife) and moved back to the U.S. Ernie then spent the next several years living in Key West, fishing, sailing around the Caribbean, getting drunk, and writing more books. He also went to Africa and shot various large animals, because nothing says "macho man" quite like shooting an elephant. In the late 1930's he worked as a war correspondent during the Spanish Civil War, where he pretty much became a communist. It was at this time that he left his second wife and married a fellow war correspondent named Martha.

The new couple made their home in Cuba where Ernie wrote more books, got drunk, went fishing, and bred six toed cats. It was also during this time that Ernie became a Soviet spy codenamed Argo, though apparently not a very good one, since he never supplied any information worth knowing. Ernie spent the early years of World War II cruising around the Caribbean on his boat claiming he was looking for Nazi submarines, but most likely just getting tanked and hiding from his wife. As American troops began to land in France, Ernie went with them as a war correspondent, even leading a small group of French militia for a time (which was against the Geneva Convention). However, he spent most of the war sick in bed. It was during this time that he left his third wife and married his fourth, a woman named Mary. After the war, the new couple moved back to Cuba where Ernie got drunk, wrote books, and machine gunned sharks for fun. Most of his books written at this time did not sell well, probably because they were all about old dudes getting it on with hot young broads. However, it was also at this time that Ernie won the Nobel Prize for his book about a sad old man who can't catch a break.

Despite some near disasters, Mary and Ernie stayed together. The pair went to Africa for a time where they got in a plane crash, then a second plane crash trying to get to the hospital, only to finally arrive to find they had been declared legally dead (which is probably why he won the Nobel Prize). Still very much alive, Ernie then went on a fishing trip where a he was severely burned in a brushfire. Ernie dealt with most of this by getting extremely drunk all the time, writing, and taking an African wife (which Mary seemed cool with). Ernie then returned to Cuba, but soon after moved to Idaho, where again, he spent all his time writing, getting drunk, and becoming increasingly paranoid that the FBI was watching him (which they were). The paranoia became so bad that Mary had Ernie go through electro-shock treatment in an attempt to cure him. It did not work. Not long after, Ernie blew his own brains out. This was a bit of a family tradition given that his father, sister, and brother all did the same. Mary dealt with Ernie's death by publishing the last of his books and becoming good friends with two of her three predecessors.

#30 John Jeremiah Johnson
Liver Eater

JJ was a giant of a man. He stood six foot two, weighed 260 pounds, and was reportedly cut like a Greek statue. In short, he was not the kind of man you wanted to fuck around with. Born to fairly boring parents in New Jersey in the early nineteenth century, JJ quickly got bored and decided it was time to skedaddle. At age sixteen he joined the navy to fight in the Mexican War, but soon got in trouble for his habit of not obeying orders and punching his superior officers. Given that the old timey navy used to hang people for such offenses, he quickly skedaddled and made his way north into the Rocky Mountains where he was adopted by a lonely old fur trapper who taught him the trade (of fur trapping that is). JJ stayed in the Rockies for most of his life, working as a fur trapper and a wood hawk, which despite the cool name just meant he cut up wood for use on steamships. Early in his career JJ married a woman of the Flathead Indian tribe, by which we mean he bought her from her father. JJ, quite happy with his new bride, built her a cabin, and then left for the winter to tend his traps. While he was gone a group of Crow Indians found the cabin and killed his wife.

JJ arrived back at the cabin in spring to find the skeletal remains of not only his wife, but also his unborn baby. Understandably upset, JJ swore revenge against all Crow and went on a twenty-five year rampage. JJ wandered the Rocky Mountains like some of kind of murderous phantom, killing any Crow he found. People wandering the mountains, both Indians and whites, reported finding slain Crow scattered hither and thither, their heads scalped, and their livers cut out and consumed. Yeah, that's right, he ate their livers. Why? Who the fuck knows. Over the two and a half decades of JJ's rampage over 300 Crow were reportedly killed, making JJ one of the most proficient serial killers in American history, you know, if Americans of the time had considered Indians people. Tales of these exploits were told around many a campfire and JJ was given the moniker Liver Eating Johnson, in part to help differentiate him from the other Johnson's of the area, which included Pear Loving Johnson and Long Toes Johnson. What's that? You've never heard of Pear Loving Johnson? Well, that's probably because nobody gives a shit about you if your only claim to fame is that you really love pears, unless I guess there was a more literal meaning.

Anyways, the Crow, decidedly upset about the wanton murder, sent their best twenty warriors to kill JJ. What exactly happened to this elite commando team is unknown, but none of them came back. The Blackfoot tribe were somewhat luckier. They managed to capture JJ by trickery. They tied him up with leather thongs and made plans to give him as a gift to the Crow. JJ, having none of that shit, ate the leather bindings, killed his guard with a single punch, and then used the guard's own knife to scalp him and cut off his leg. JJ then used the unfortunate guard's severed leg as a club to battle his way out of the village. It was a 200 mile journey to safety, one JJ made in the dead of winter, surviving by eating the leg, which he also used to kill a cougar. Some might question why JJ didn't just eat the cougar, but then again, such questions are usually reserved for sane people.

After the whole eating a leg thing, JJ took a short break from serial killing to join the Union Army and fight in the Civil War as a sharpshooter. After the war he went back to killing Crow until he finally got bored and declared a treaty. The Crow were decidedly okay with this. Vengeance had been done, and besides, JJ had gotten into the whiskey peddling business and living Crow drank significantly more whiskey than dead ones. JJ continued to live in the Rockies for some time, even being appointed a deputy sheriff and then a town marshal in Montana for a time. When JJ turned seventy-five he apparently decided it was time to die. He wandered his way westward to Los Angeles, for god only knows what reason, and died in a veteran's home a month later. Seventy-four years later, a group of students successfully got his remains relocated to Wyoming, which from the surviving Crow's point of view, was probably not all that awesome.

#31 John Harvey Kellogg
A Bit of a Flake

Harvey had a lot of things going for him. He was a highly respected medical doctor, a creative thinker, an upstanding member of the Seventh Day Adventist Church, and the head of the Battle Creek Sanitarium, one of the most respected sanitariums of the late nineteenth century. However, his life would have probably been better if he hadn't been so obsessed with sex and colons.

You might recognize Harvey's name from your box of breakfast cereal. Harvey and his brother Willy were the inventors of corn flakes. However, even this small invention caused turmoil in Harvey's life. Harvey, a staunch Grahamite, believed that all foods should be as bland as possible, since delicious food apparently caused sexual excitement, which Harvey viewed as a negative for some reason. Willy held the opposing view that sugar needed to be added because corn flakes tasted like cardboard. The rift caused the brothers to found competing companies, which was further complicated when C.W. Post, a former patient of Harvey's, began making his own identical corn flakes. So yeah, the entire dry cereal aisle was created by sexually repressed nut jobs. Speaking of nuts, Harvey wasn't just nuts, he was also really into nuts, like a squirrel. Harvey, a staunch vegetarian, believed that nuts would save the world from hunger, a fact he had no problem telling anyone within earshot.

Additionally, his obsession with sex was never what you could call a healthy one, and by that, we mean it wasn't healthy for anybody else. Harvey got married at a young age, but refused to consummate the relationship. This upset his wife somewhat in that she had been hoping to have children. Harvey, ever a creative man, solved the problem by adopting forty-two orphans. All in all, his wife was the lucky one. Harvey had it in his head that sex that caused any kind of pleasure was most detrimental to one's health. However, even worse was masturbating. Those vile souls that dared to touch their own genitals were doomed to blindness, degrading mental faculties, urinary diseases, cancer of the womb, and epilepsy. In Harvey's own words countless people were "dying by their own hand." To battle this national health epidemic, Harvey, as a medical doctor, adopted increasingly severe methods. It started with the bandaging and tying of hands, which was followed by patented groin cages and electrical shocks. When these methods didn't work, Harvey began sewing foreskins shut, then reversed his opinion and began circumcising boys (that's boys, not babies) without anesthetic. Oh, and don't you worry, he didn't forget the gentler sex. Girls were given a nice drop of carbolic acid on the clitoris, and in more severe cases, the clitoris was just cut off.

When not mutilating genitals, Harvey stayed busy running one of America's most successful and famous sanitariums. Some of the most famous people of the time visited Battle Creek, including President Taft. Upon arrival all patients had to provide Harvey with a stool sample, which he personally inspected to judge the health of his "victims". Each patient was then given an enema by a device that would rapidly instill several gallons of water in an alarmingly short amount of time. With their intestines squeaky clean, patients would then be given a course of yogurt, half of which was eaten, with the other half shoved up their ass. Every day Harvey's patients were put through a series of breathing exercises and meal time marches to aid in digestion. Harvey was also a big fan of both hydrotherapy (basically early day hot tubs) and phototherapy (sitting under heat lamps), both of which sound fairly benign, but again, Harvey was a creative man. To save time he built a radiant heat bath, which was a hot tub full of electric heat lamps. These baths were popular, though strangely quite a few people died of electrocution. Of course, not everything was bad. Harvey was also big on not smoking in a time when everyone was pretty onboard with it, so you know, being right one out of a hundred times ain't that bad.

As time went on Harvey's health claims slowly went out of vogue, which all together was a bit of a good thing, except for the whole anti-smoking part. Though Harvey continued running a sanitarium until his death, as he aged he became more involved with other causes. One of these was the belief that god resided in everything, and therefore everything should be worshipped like god, a belief that got him kicked out of the Seventh Day Adventists. He also became a major supporter of eugenics, calling for racial segregation and the ending of immigration to preserve the all important American gene pool. Though today largely regarded to be a nut, Harvey did live to be ninety-one. Enjoy your fucking corn flakes.

#32 Anthony Comstock
The Smasher of Smut

Tony was not the kind of guy anyone enjoyed hanging out with. To call him boring would be a little bit of an understatement. The man's idea of a dirty joke involved two pigs sitting together in the mud. His claimed view of a perfect day involved strolling through a meadow discussing the bible, though in reality it probably more involved sticking his nose where it was none of his business. He didn't drink, smoke, gamble, or do any kind of vice whatsoever. A veteran of the Civil War, Tony's biggest complaint of military life was all the profanity. You've probably never heard of this kill-joy, but it is sufficient to say that he had a greater effect on censorship than any other American.

To be fair to Tony, it wasn't like he had that great of a start. Born and raised in an ultra-conservative household, Tony found himself living in a world that was making him decidedly uncomfortable. The America of the late nineteenth and early twentieth centuries was a rapidly changing place. Old Victorian ideals were beginning to give way to more liberal views towards art, sex, and women's rights. At first, Tony had little to do with any of this. He seemed mostly content to support his young family and work at the Young Men's Christian Association (YMCA), which at the time did not have certain connotations suggested by the popular song by the Village People. However, after his only child died in infancy, Tony seemed to completely lose his shit. Grief can express itself in many ways. For Tony his grief expressed itself via a declaration of war on moral corruption.

Tony became a founding member of the New York Society for the Suppression of Vice (NYSSV), which soon became famous for its work to suppress and ban any literary works it considered smutty. Supported by the YMCA, Tony and the NYSSV roamed the streets of New York, monitoring newsstands for anything indecent. In cases where smut was found, the dealers were quickly handed over to the proper authorities, who in thanks gave the NYSSV half of all fines levied as a result. However, these early attempts did little to prevent the promulgation of smut, most of which traveled via the mail. Tony, fully aware of this, began concentrating his energies into politics. For some reason, few of the politicians of the day wanted to be branded the protectors of perverts, the result being that Tony got what would become known as the Comstock Act passed through Congress. The Comstock Act made it illegal for anyone to mail erotica, contraceptives, abortion aids, sex toys, any materials with information regarding the previous, and even personal letters alluding to any sexual content. To top it all off, Tony was given a position with the postal service as a special inspector, giving him the ability to go through people's mail as he pleased.

Given that at the time the Comstock Act was in effect, everything was mailed, this meant that nearly everything was censored in the U.S. For Tony, the removal of smut was a matter of life and death. In his view, smut led to a moral degradation which in turn led to venereal diseases, alcoholism, and drug addiction. What exactly was smut you might ask? Well, it was pretty much whatever Tony decided was smut, and his view on the matter was quite broad to the level that he even banned the mailing of anatomy textbooks. Literature, plays, art, and science - none of it was safe from Tony's prudish wrath. He quickly became the bane of most of the early civil liberties groups, but the darling of most of the church groups. Regardless of what anybody thought of him, it does have to be admitted that Tony was a clever son of a bitch. One of his favorite tactics was to, while pretending to be someone else, order lascivious items through the mail, only to have the senders arrested soon after the items' arrival. Over time Tony's investigations grew to include not just the distribution of pornography and contraceptives, but also women's rights materials and items related to commercial fraud. Tony called himself "the weeder in God's garden".

Over the four decades of Tony's career it is believed that he destroyed 15 tons of books, 284,000 pounds of plates used for printing, and nearly 4 million pictures. Tony also liked to boast that he was responsible for 4,000 arrests and 15 suicides. Many people chose to kill themselves rather than face the shame of a public trial, amongst them a prominent abortionist and the author of the first marriage manual. For a time, J. Edgar Hoover studied under Tony to learn about his methods. Late in life Tony was bashed over the head by an anonymous attacker. This attack only made him more zealous in his cause. Tony died at the age of seventy-one, unable to hold back the steadily rising tide of smut. Throughout the 1920's and 1930's, court cases struck down the Comstock Act bit by bit. However, the last parts weren't repealed until the 1970's.

#33 Zelda Fitzgerald
The Great Gatsby's Gal

Zelda was born to a rich southern family at the start of the twentieth century. Her mother was a southern belle and her father was a remote and strict man. Both doted on and spoiled Zelda, an active girl who enjoyed swimming, the outdoors, and ballet. As she blossomed into a teenager she became quite wild for the time: drinking, smoking, and spending all of her time in the company of various boys. She hungered for the attention of others and did anything to attract it; things like dancing the Charleston (it was a very different time) and wearing flesh covered swimsuits so people thought she swam naked. Through it all her reputation never suffered thanks to the facts that she was extremely attractive and her family was very wealthy. Zelda first met F. Scott Fitzgerald when she was eighteen and he was twenty-four. Scott was stationed at a nearby military base and was a self-assured man who dreamed of being an author. The two fell in love, but Zelda refused to marry Scott because he was unattractively impoverished. To correct this, Scott simply wrote his first book which made him an overnight success. Scott swept Zelda away to New York City and the two were soon married.

Scott and Zelda were the toast of New York, or rather the toast of the city's most famous drunks. Their lives, despite Prohibition, revolved around never ending parties fueled by an unquenchable thirst for booze. They'd go to parties and drink until they passed out. They'd swim in public fountains, get thrown out of hotels, and pass out in random houses. The newspapers loved them. Soon after the publication of Scott's second novel, Zelda gave birth to a daughter who was quickly handed off to a series of nannies and boarding schools. The next year Zelda became pregnant again, but got an abortion in order to save her figure. Behind the couple's public facade was a shit show of bitter fights, heavy drinking, and rampant spending. With Scott's writing career on the rocks, the two moved to France where Scott concentrated on his writing and Zelda concentrated on an affair with a French pilot. Before long Zelda demanded a divorce, which Scott dealt with by locking her in the house until she changed her mind. Though Scott soon published his third and most famous novel, *The Great Gatsby*, things quickly fell apart from there. Zelda tried to kill herself with sleeping pills and Scott double downed on his alcoholism.

Zelda got back at her husband by telling him that she disliked having sex with him because he had a tiny penis and was most likely a homosexual. This prompted him to show his penis to Ernest Hemingway for his opinion. Scott sought revenge by having sex with a prostitute, which somehow proved his masculinity. Upon discovering this, Zelda purposefully threw herself down a flight of stairs at a party, but her husband pretended not to notice. The two became increasingly miserable. Scott's writing wasn't going well and Zelda was decidedly bored and lonely, which she coped with by doing crazy antics to get Scott's attention, which he dealt with by guzzling booze. For a while Zelda took back up ballet dancing, practicing herself into physical and mental exhaustion every day, but Scott called it a waste of time because of her age. The two still partied, but fewer people wanted to be around them. Zelda became increasingly erratic until Scott finally had her shut up in a looney bin. The headshrinkers there diagnosed her with schizophrenia. It was around this time that they moved back to America, with Zelda transferring to a better, more American mental institution soon after their return.

Zelda's time as a crazy person wasn't wasted. She wrote a book which enraged her husband since she used many tales from her own life. Scott believed that if anybody was going to write about Zelda's insanity and his alcoholism it was going to be him. The book didn't sell well, nor did the many art pieces that Zelda painted. Over the next several years Scott finished his fourth novel, but spent most of his time living in Hollywood, having an affair with another woman and taking any writing job he could get to help pay for his wife's medical bills. Zelda meanwhile underwent numerous shock therapies, completely lost her mind, and started having conversations with many long dead historical figures. Near broke, the pair continued in a strange love-hate relationship for the rest of their lives, barely ever seeing each other. Their last time together was a vacation to Cuba where Scott was beaten up for trying to stop a cockfight and became so intoxicated and exhausted that he had to be hospitalized. Two years later he died at the age of forty-four. Zelda, newly released from the insane asylum, missed both his funeral and her daughter's wedding. She soon returned to the familiar comfort of the asylum where she died at the age of forty-seven when it burnt to the ground.

#34 Florence Foster Jenkins
The World's Worst Opera Singer

Flo was born to rich parents in the late nineteenth century and grew up with a silver spoon in her mouth. She learned to love the stage at an early age. A bit of a piano prodigy, she performed at many society events starting at age seven, culminating with playing for President Hayes at the White House. After graduating from high school she told her father that she wanted to go to Europe to study music. Her father, not a fan of the arts, told her she would be better off marrying a doctor. Not liking this answer, Flo ran off and eloped with a doctor of poor reputation named Frank Jenkins, who, thanks to his love of hookers, gave her syphilis. Upon discovering this, Flo left Frank, though a divorce was never formalized. For a period of time she tried to make it on her own as a pianist, giving piano lessons to support herself, but an arm injury put an end to those dreams and she eventually moved in with her mother in New York City. It was here that she met an Englishman seven years her junior, named St. Clair Bayfield, who also happened to be a failed Shakespearean actor. The two became unofficially married and lived in a strange cohabitation which involved them never sleeping together (because of the syphilis) and St. Clair keeping an apartment and girlfriend on the side.

Before long, Flo's father died, leaving her a fat inheritance. Flo, deciding to restart her musical career, began taking voice lessons and immersing herself in New York's high society. She joined dozens of social organizations and even started her own music club, the Verdi Club (giving herself the title President Soprano Hostess) where she staged lavish tableau's, most of which cast her as a main character, wearing extremely elaborate costumes she designed herself. Flo was generous with her money, donating to most of the major musical and artistic endeavors of the city for the next forty years, and earning the great love and admiration of high society. However, her great dream was to become a singer, a dream largely limited by the fact that the woman couldn't sing worth a shit. This isn't an overstatement. The woman sounded like the death cries of a screaming bird in the mouth of a cat suffering from laryngitis. She had no sense of rhythm, timing, pitch, or tone. She was consistently flat and often mispronounced many of the words she was singing. To make it all worse she always chose to sing operatic solos far beyond her technical abilities and vocal range. It was distorted and terrible, and Flo had no idea.

She first started singing in her forties and it wasn't too long before she began hosting private concerts at her apartment and at small clubs. Attendance was by personal invitation only, restricted to a select group of friends and club members. Strangers and music critics were always excluded. Her friends, who loved her dearly, treated her performances as the highest of arts, and in the rare cases where someone broke into laughter, which invariably happened at every recital, they cheered loudly to cover it up. It was a grand world created by the willingness of people to lie to her and Flo's willingness to lie to herself. She truly enjoyed singing and the stage more than anything else, and saw herself as equal to many of the great opera singers of the day. To be fair to Flo, it is highly likely that her syphilis, and its treatment with mercury and arsenic, caused at least partial hearing loss and perhaps some mental instability. It was madness, but a madness that everyone was willing to go along with as long as the money kept flowing. Few people in history can claim the devotion Flo created amongst her friends and fans.

The mystery surrounding Flo's recitals drove the New York art scene insane. Anything so private as her shows was sure to cause a clamor. At age seventy-six Flo finally gave into public demand and agreed to do a show at Carnegie Hall. Tickets sold out weeks in advance. Numerous celebrities attended. At the height of World War II it was the musical event of the season. Flo, in one of her own wardrobe creations, took the stage. As the audience fell quiet with anticipation, Flo began to sing, and complete pandemonium broke out. The audience broke out into laughter, applause, and cheering. People had to be carried out due to becoming too hysterical. Throughout it all Flo kept going, basking in the attention. Though the audience was kind to her, the critics were not. The scathing reviews of what turned out to be her only public concert hurt Flo deeply. Within a month she died of a heart attack.

#35 Linda Hazzard
Fast Ways to Get Healthy

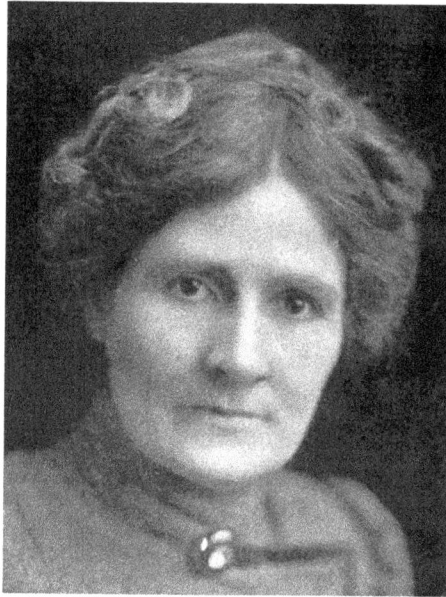

Linda's life started the same as most women's of the early nineteenth century, marrying a relative stranger at the age of eighteen to start pumping out kids. However, this life wasn't for Linda. She had dreams of becoming a doctor, and so, at age 31 she divorced her husband, abandoned her children, and moved to Minneapolis. Now, becoming a doctor is quite difficult, what with all the schooling, studying, internships, and licensing exams. Not wanting to deal with any of that bullshit, Linda instead decided to go into natural medicine and became a proponent of fasting to clear toxins from the body. She killed her first patient at the turn of the century. She was arrested, but the Minnesota courts found that since she wasn't licensed to practice medicine they couldn't hold her accountable. Now most people would look at this turn of events and think about re-evaluating their lives. Linda was not one of these people. Instead she started pursuing a man named Sam Hazzard, whom she decided was the love of her life despite him being a drunkard who had been discharged from the army for forgery and embezzling, and oh yes, he was also married. Not caring about any of these things, Linda convinced Sam to marry her. Surprisingly, he was soon arrested for bigamy and consequently imprisoned for two years.

While Sam rotted in jail, Linda spent her time writing a book on fasting which gained her national recognition. As soon as Sam was released, the two moved to the Puget Sound area where they opened up a sanitarium in order to put Linda's beliefs into practice. She believed that all diseases were caused by toxins that built up in the body and that the only way to remove the toxins was to abstain from eating until they were flushed out. Treatment at the sanitarium involved only eating a thin vegetable broth, daily enemas which could last hours at a time, and massages that more closely resembled beatings. On some occasions, these treatments could last for months. Despite the fact that Linda was quite literally starving people to death, the rich and well to do flocked to her to heal their ills. Many of those who went through the treatment reported an energy and exuberance they had never felt before, but only after they started eating again. People in the area, who watched the emaciated patients stumble through their daily morning exercises, nicknamed the sanitarium Starvation Heights. In four years at least fourteen people died, many of whom mysteriously gifted much of their fortunes to the sanitarium.

Things finally came to a head when wealthy British sisters and hypochondriacs Dorothea and Claire Williamson checked into the sanitarium. Claire died of starvation a few weeks later and Dorothea was declared mentally incapable fell and under Linda's guardianship. Help arrived in the form of an old family friend from Australia who was greeted by Linda, wearing Claire's clothes and jewels. The family friend was then shown what she was told was Claire's body, which looked nothing like her, and then taken to see Dorothea, who by this time only weighed 50 pounds. Linda refused to free Dorothea until her bills were paid. The family friend responded by having Linda arrested for murder. The trial that followed was as insane as everything else. Linda declared that she was being persecuted by the patriarchy and the Big Traditional Medicine industry. Natural medicine and women's groups flocked to her aid, some of whom threatened witnesses and ransacked houses and law offices. Linda declared that the people had died due to being full of too many toxins to cure. The court declared her guilty and had her imprisoned for manslaughter.

After two years in the clink Linda was released. She and her husband Sam hastily moved to New Zealand to be closer to a group of ardent supporters. Here, she wrote another book about not eating, declared herself a dietitian and a physician, and starved more people to death with her quack ideas. While in New Zealand she was arrested for practicing medicine without a license, but was released by paying a fine, which would work out to $450 in today's money. Over the next decade she became quite wealthy, which allowed her to return to the Puget Sound area and reopen her sanitarium. The sanitarium operated for another fifteen years before finally burning down. Throughout this period, despite state officials claiming they were keeping an eye on it, numerous more people starved themselves to death, believing that they were making themselves healthier. Given all this one might ask themselves why people would continue to seek Linda's quack treatments. The answer is simple, people were just as stupid then as they are today. In her early seventies, Linda fell ill, so naturally, she prescribed her own treatment to herself and starved to death.

#36 Daniel Sickles
One Legged Cocksman

Danny, often called Devil Dan, was born to a well to do New York family that had just enough money for Danny to be a crazy as balls jack ass. Danny got himself a good university education and then tried a couple of jobs over the years, including printer and lawyer, before deciding that working was for schmucks. Like many people who don't want to work for a living, he ran for public office, getting himself elected to the New York legislature. To celebrate, he attached himself to Fanny White, one of the highest of high class prostitutes in New York City at the time. Their relationship lasted seven years. Fanny did not consider Danny a customer, but rather her paramour, which for Danny worked out quite well considering it meant he did not have to pay her. Danny returned the favor by openly parading her around town and taking her to all sorts of official government meetings and parties. Being Victorian times, this caused a bit of a scandal, which was further exacerbated when it came to light that Fanny and her brothel money had funded his re-election campaign. At the age of 33, and not wanting to get a real job, Danny solved the problem by marrying a 15 year old girl named Teresa Bagioli, a move he defended by stating that Teresa was sophisticated for her age and spoke five languages. In case none of this creeps you out enough he had also known the girl since she was an infant. Fanny, somewhat displeased with the match, publicly beat Danny with a horsewhip.

Shortly thereafter Danny was sent to work at the U.S. embassy in London. Not one to let social norms influence him, left his new child bride in New York, though she was already pregnant, and instead took his prostitute Fanny. He then proceeded to introduce her to Queen Victoria, using a political opponent's last name as her alias. Danny's bosses, less than amused, forced him to get rid of Fanny and send for his wife. However, he ended up snubbing Queen Victoria at an Independence Day celebration and was sent home. When Danny returned to New York he got himself elected to the state legislature again. He and his wife then spent the next several years getting drunk at parties during which time

Teresa began having an affair with Philip Barton Key, the son of the guy who wrote the Star Spangled Banner. When Danny found out about the affair, he flew into a rage, shooting and killing his rival in broad daylight across the street from the White House. He then calmly walked to the Attorney General's house and surrendered. The trial was a total shit show, with Danny claiming temporary insanity, the first time such a defense was ever used. The newspapers went wild over the story, calling Danny a hero for saving the women of America from Key's dick. While in prison, Danny was given preferential treatment, including receiving numerous visitors and being allowed to pack a pistol. He even got a personal letter from the president. The icing on the cake was when he publicly forgave his wife. Of course, he was found innocent.

When the Civil War broke out Danny used his political connections to get himself appointed a general. However, he spent most of the early years of the war hanging out in Washington D.C., drinking beer, and sleeping with prostitutes. Danny got along well with his superior officer, General Joe Hooker, a man who loved boozing and whoring so much that his surname became a term for prostitute. Between the two of them they pretty much ran a brothel/bar in the command tent. Unfortunately for Danny, Joe Hooker got canned for being a drunken whore monger, and was replaced by General George Meade, a man who considered reading the bible a heck of a good time. They of course didn't get along and Danny did his best to ignore all of Meade's orders. In the Battle of Gettysburg, Danny disobeyed orders and moved his troops forward into a vulnerable position. In the ensuing battle the brigade was slaughtered and Danny lost a leg to a cannonball, which led to him being one of the first people to arrive back in Washington D.C. after the battle. In D.C. Danny declared that Meade was a little bitch and that his own actions had led to victory for the Union. He also donated his shattered leg to a museum, which he visited every year on the anniversary of losing it.

After the Civil War, Danny stayed in the army and oversaw Reconstruction in South Carolina, during which time his wife Teresa died of tuberculosis. Danny was then made ambassador to Spain, an appointment he apparently assumed meant sleeping with half of the Spanish royal court, including the queen. When Danny wasn't screwing the better looking half of the Spanish nobility, he kept himself busy by writing inaccurate and emotional letters to his superiors calling for war between the two countries. Luckily these letters were largely ignored. Growing bored with fucking a queen, Danny married her maid, Carmina Creagh, a woman twenty years his junior, and fathered two kids, all of whom he left in Spain when he returned to the U.S. Back in the states, Danny got himself re-elected to public office and spent the rest of his life trying to convince people that he was a god damn war hero. This included playing an important role in the efforts to preserve the Gettysburg battlefield. Thirty-four years after the Battle of Gettysburg, he was finally awarded the Medal of Honor, the highest medal a soldier can be given, though it was probably just given to him to get him to shut the fuck up. Danny died at the age of 94. You can still see his leg today at the Army Medical Museum in Washington D.C.

#37 Fanny White
The Whore with A Lot of Gold

Fanny was not the kind of girl you imagined growing up to be a prostitute. Raised on a small farm in upstate New York she received a fine education and was reported to be a bookish girl, which is a nice old timey way of calling her a nerd. Unfortunately for Fanny, her probable life of milking cows and making babies until she died was derailed at age eighteen when she became the victim of a seducer. In old fashioned times a seducer was a man who seduced "naive" young women with the promise of marriage in order to get into their pants. Many a young woman, understandably a little anxious after years of sexual repression, jumped the gun a bit on the honeymoon portion, only to find their would be husbands running off to the hills. Now to the modern day sophisticate, this may sound mildly unfortunate, but not world ending. Unfortunately, in the Victorian era such abandoned women were considered ruined, like a bruised peach, and no respectable man or woman of the time wanted anything to do with a damaged peach. In fact, this was such a problem that it later led to the development of engagement rings. So, there you go ladies, not only is your ring probably mined by slave children, it also represents a time when women were thought of the same as a piece of fruit. Way to hold onto that tradition.

With her reputation totally fucked, Fanny fled to live with her brother in New York City, where she got a shitty job cleaning hotel rooms. However, her brother, probably worried that bruised peach syndrome was contagious or something, kicked her out a short time later. With nowhere else to go she moved into a brothel and became a whore, where her societal status was more of an attribute than a detriment. The mid-1800's was a particularly unpleasant time to be a prostitute, not that it really ever is, what with the rampant tuberculosis and syphilis. On the plus side, most brothels were owned by women, which seems kind of like common sense since putting a man in charge of a brothel is like having your kids guard the jar of cookies; it just doesn't work. Luckily for Fanny, she had a good head on her shoulders, unaffected by the ravages of syphilis, and within four years she owned the brothel where she worked. Not content with her low standing she began to live the good life, taking a New York politician named Danny Sickles as her paramour. A paramour was a man a prostitute considered herself to be in a relationship with. She didn't charge him money, but he did give her a lot of really nice gifts, which makes it totally different. Danny took her to all sorts of fancy dinners and parties, much to the chagrin of the other guests.

Fanny, what with her head for numbers, continued to grow her business, starting a high class brothel for rich merchants, politicians, and foreign dignitaries. She also gave away freebies to the local police for reasons that can only be described as obvious. The only run in with the law she had was when she was arrested for walking around dressed as a man, which apparently was worse than fucking strangers for money. Fanny also funded one of Danny's re-election campaigns, which caused a big enough scandal that he married a fifteen year old girl (which totally makes sense). Fanny, pissed as hell, beat him with a horsewhip in the lobby of a fancy hotel. However, Danny got back into her good graces, and into the rest of her presumably, by taking her to England with him instead of his young bride. In London, Fanny openly accompanied Danny to theaters, operas, and diplomatic events. She even got Danny to present her to Queen Victoria, though under the assumed surname of one Danny's political rivals. Danny's superiors, less than amused with all this, forced him to break up with Fanny soon after. Brokenhearted, Fanny then went on a tour of Europe, visiting aristocratic resorts and sleeping with aristocrats, until she was forcefully removed from a Paris Opera for making a drunken scene. She then returned to New York and opened a second brothel.

Upon returning home Fanny decided that she would try her hand at not being a whore anymore, so set her sights on finding a respectable husband. After a few false starts she finally met her goal with a lawyer, seven years her junior, named Eddie Blankman. For Eddie, Fanny might have been a whore, but by god, she was a rich whore. Now miraculously respectable, Fanny proceeded to lavish the family that had abandoned her all those years ago with a multitude of gifts, even paying for her niece's schooling. However, she refused to sign any of her property over to her new husband, because her life had made her no fool, though the fact that he tried to fuck her niece also probably had something to do with it. Unfortunately for Fanny, her life as a respectable woman was not to last long. She died at the age of 37 of internal bleeding. Her family, convinced that her dick of a husband poisoned her, had her dug up and examined several times to try and find proof, but none was ever found. It is estimated that Fanny was worth around $2 million in today's money at the time of her death. After a lengthy legal battle that went clear to the state supreme court, Eddie inherited everything.

#38 Claudette Colvin
The Spark That Wasn't Quite Right

If it has to be explained to you that being black in America has been fairly shitty for pretty much all of our history, then buddy, you're a bit of a fricking moron. In the constant struggle of two steps forward and one step back, one courageous woman from Montgomery, Alabama was brave enough in the mid-1950's to say she wasn't going to take anymore bullshit. That woman's name was Claudette Colvin. What? You thought I was going to say Rosa Parks? You don't know who Claudette is? Well buddy, better sit down, because history is always shittier than most books would have you believe.

Claudette was born and raised in Montgomery right in the heart of the segregated south. Now, segregation was at the time a legally protected system theoretically based on the idea of "separate, but equal", though in every case "equal" meant that blacks got everything whites did, just in a much shittier, both figuratively and literally, form. When it came to the city bus system, everyone rode the same bus, because even racists prefer profits over ideology. However, blacks had to sit in the back, and if a white person needed their seat they had to stand. This was the world that Claudette grew up in, and this was the world that, at the age of sixteen, she decided she wouldn't put up with anymore. In March of 1955, a full nine months before Rosa Parks, Claudette, on her way home from school, refused to give up her seat to a white woman. Screaming that it was her constitutional right not to get up for anyone, Claudette was forced from the bus and arrested.

Now comes the part where things begin to get rather fucked up. The NAACP had been looking for someone just like Claudette for several years. You see, while most people like to imagine political activism as massive world changing protests, the real change tends to come from groups of well funded lawyers finding court cases to push up through the judicial system. If this sounds tedious as hell, you're right, it is, and one of the most important things in the process is that the right symbol is found. Unfortunately for Claudette she did not fit this bill. Claudette was from a poor family and was best described as mouthy, emotional, and feisty, as most teenagers are. Unlike most teenagers, she was also pregnant with the bastard child of a married man. However, these weren't the biggest knocks against her. The biggest knock was that she was considered too black. That's right, the NAACP wanted a black woman who would create more national sympathy, which is a real nice way of saying she had to look whiter. Over the next nine months four more women were arrested for not giving up their seats, and all four were rejected by the NAACP for a myriad of reasons, which were largely cover for the fact that they were all too black.

By December of 1955, the NAACP was tired of waiting for a champion, so they made their own in the form of the secretary of the NAACP's Montgomery chapter, Rosa Parks. Rosa was 42, from a middle class family, calm, well mannered, and most importantly, had relatively straighter hair and a lighter skin tone. Rosa got on the bus, refused to give up her seat, the Montgomery Bus Boycott began, and as they say, the rest is history. Except no, things continued to be just as fucked up. The NAACP had its perfect public face, which they preserved by never letting Rosa speak in public. It should probably be mentioned that most of the Civil Rights leaders of the time were rather sexist, this being the 1950's and all. Unfortunately, Rosa's court case quickly got mired down in the local court system. The bus boycott couldn't last forever, since after all, even in the pursuit of freedom people still needed to make money to feed their families, and Rosa's case looked like it wouldn't go anywhere for years. So what did the NAACP do? I'll tell you what. They went back to all the women they had rejected, including Claudette, and started a civil case that skipped right to the federal level. This case quickly worked its way up to the U.S. Supreme Court, which ruled in December of 1956 that all buses had to be desegregated. It was one of the first great victories of the Civil Rights Movement.

So that's it, right? Happy ending? Not really. During and after the court case, Claudette and the other five women found themselves targeted for retribution via harassment, an inability to find work, and even death threats. The NAACP, having gotten what it wanted, did little to help them. Claudette was forced to move to New York in 1958 where she worked in a nursing home and had a second bastard child. Claudette, as well as the other women who were all considered too black, disappeared into anonymity, their contribution almost entirely forgotten.

#39 Audrey Munson
The Living Statue

Hardly anyone remembers who Audrey is today, but there's a damn good chance that you've seen her face, not to mention all the rest of her. Audrey wasn't born with much. Her parents decidedly lacked in the financial department, a situation made worse by their divorce when Audrey was in her early teens. Soon after the divorce, Audrey's mother took her daughter to New York City, where she hoped to capitalize on Audrey's assets, namely her daughter's exquisitely proportioned lithe body and perfectly symmetrical face. The girl was pretty much the embodiment of a Greek statue. When reading the last few sentences did your mind instantly go to prostitution? If so, don't worry, in this case exploitation only meant forcing a 15 year old girl to lie about her age and audition as a chorus girl for low budget Broadway plays. See? Much better. Audrey, though good looking, was not a very good dancer, but did manage to land enough roles to keep her and her mother off the street.

Things changed for the teenage Audrey in 1906 when a well known photographer noticed her walking down the street one day, and becoming totally enamored with her, begged for the opportunity to take pictures of her. If that sounds creepy, another story claims that the photographer accidentally hit Audrey with his car, and then wanted to take her picture. Either way, needing the money, Audrey (and her mother) agreed. The photographer then showed the photographs, again pictures of a teenage girl, to a sculptor friend who also became enamored with her. The sculptor then hired Audrey to model for a few statues he wanted to create. This being the art world, he of course asked her to pose nude. Again, needing the money, Audrey and her mother agreed. The statues were such a big hit that it wasn't long before other artists also began seeking Audrey out for her "talents", and thus a career of standing around naked was born.

Over the next decade Audrey was the model for hundreds of statues and monuments, most of them nude. The majority of these could be found in New York City, but many others were spread across the country from one coast to the other. The culmination of her career was the Panama-Pacific International Exposition in San Francisco, a world's fair which celebrated the opening of the Panama Canal in 1915. Three quarters of the statues and carvings at the exposition were graced by her image. She gained international notoriety and thousands of love letters and marriage proposals poured in from around the world. To capitalize on her success, Audrey moved to Hollywood to become an actress in the newly established silent film industry. There was just one problem with this plan, Audrey couldn't act worth shit. However, she was willing to take off all of her clothes, becoming the first woman to do so in a movie that wasn't a porn. As an aside, the advent of the moving pornographic picture began pretty much the moment the movie camera was invented. This sans clothes willingness got her parts in four movies, though she only did the nude bits, with stunt doubles doing all the acting.

Despite all the fame, Audrey was not so good with money. It seemed to flow out as quickly as it flowed in. Her Hollywood career fell apart after a few years, a fact she blamed on a jilted suitor who she reported to the government for being a German sympathizer. She and her mother then moved into a boarding house run by a nice doctor. However, the doctor fell in love with Audrey and soon murdered his wife to prove it. The press coverage effectively ended her career at the age of 28. Audrey and her mother moved to upstate New York where they made a living selling silverware door to door. Over the next several years the decline in Audrey's fame and fortune led to a deterioration in her mental health. After a failed attempt to commit suicide she became delusional and paranoid. Finally, at age of 40, Audrey's mother had her committed into an insane asylum. She remained there for the rest of her life, forgotten, even by her family, until being re-discovered by a niece when she was in her nineties. Audrey died in the asylum at the age of 105 in 1996.

#40 Joseph Palmer
Bearded Man Extraordinaire

Once upon a time there was a pretty good guy named Joe who was considered a pillar of his community in Massachusetts. A farmer who had fought in the War of 1812, Joe was a deeply religious man who wanted to do whatever he could to be closer to god. For whatever reason in his mid-30's, Joe decided that this meant growing a big greasy hobo beard. After all, every picture of Jesus showed him wearing a beard, so for a god fearing man, beards were obviously where it was at. Now at this point you're probably thinking to yourself, "so what, it's just a damn beard". Well, for whatever reason at that time in American history nobody wore beards. In fact, nobody of any respectability had worn a beard in over a century. To the good people of Massachusetts, the sudden appearance of Joe's bearded visage amongst them came as quite a shock, and this being before the time one could just post angry Facebook rants, they of course dealt with it by being as shitty as possible directly to his face. People harassed Joe on the street, ministers refused to serve him the holy communion, and children threw rocks at him. The town even gave him a nickname, "The Old Jew", because of course people who treat a man like shit just for wearing a beard aren't that accepting of other religions. Despite the abuse, Joe steadfastly refused to shave.

Things came to a head in 1830 when four men armed with scissors and razors attempted to forcefully shave off Joe's beard. Joe managed to fight them off with his pocket knife, wounding two of the men, but was then arrested for assault. Joe refused to pay the small fine levied by a judge, so was instead thrown in prison. Life in jail wasn't easy for Joe, because even in prison a guy with a beard was just considered the lowest of the low. The guards, being sadistic sons of bitches, beat him, starved him, and locked him in solitary confinement for long periods of time. When not being harassed by the guards, Joe was attacked by his fellow inmates, who on several occasions tried to forcefully shave his beard. Through it all Joe persevered by sneaking letters out of the prison describing his trials and tribulations which were then published in local newspapers because the editors thought the whole thing was rather funny.

After fifteen months of these shenanigans, the local politicians decided that they'd had enough of old crazy bearded Joe making everyone involved in the prison system look like assholes. Joe's sentence, which again, was just because he was wearing a beard, was commuted, and he was told he was a free man. However, Joe rather enjoyed his celebrity status and so refused to go. The politicians tried several tricks to get him to leave, even bringing a letter from his 80 year old mother, but still Joe refused. Finally, out of other options, the prison guards tied Joe to a chair and forced him to accept his freedom. Joe and his beard spent the next several years lecturing across the country about prison reform and the abolition of slavery, reveling in his new found popularity.

In 1843, like many celebrities of the time, Joe joined a commune called Fruitlands, founded by none other than Ralph Waldo Emerson and Amos Bronson Alcott (father of American author Louisa May Alcott). The commune hoped to create a utopia where people subsisted on just fruit and water. Fruitlands was not exactly the success that its founders hoped it would be, mostly because the men were all a bunch of poets who had no idea how to farm, and even if they did, they saw their role as debaters of philosophy while the women did all of the actual work. Mysteriously a number of the women started to disappear. Joe, being somewhat of a clever bastard, and one of the few who actually knew how to farm, spent all of his time out in the fields with the women, where he was free to sample the fruits of his labor as he would. When the commune failed the following year, Joe bought the land and remained there the rest of his life, his popularity and fame declining rapidly in the 1860's when beards came back into fashion.

Want more Professor Errare? Are you still thirsty for knowledge? Professor Errare runs a weekly updated Facebook page of the same name with all sorts of tidbits for your perusing. You can find it here:

https://www.facebook.com/professorerrare

or at

https://www.shawnwcampbell.com/errare

Also check out Professor Errare's first book, *45 Jerks and Counting*, a pretty good yarn about how every American president in history has been a real class A jerk in one way another. It's available on Amazon.

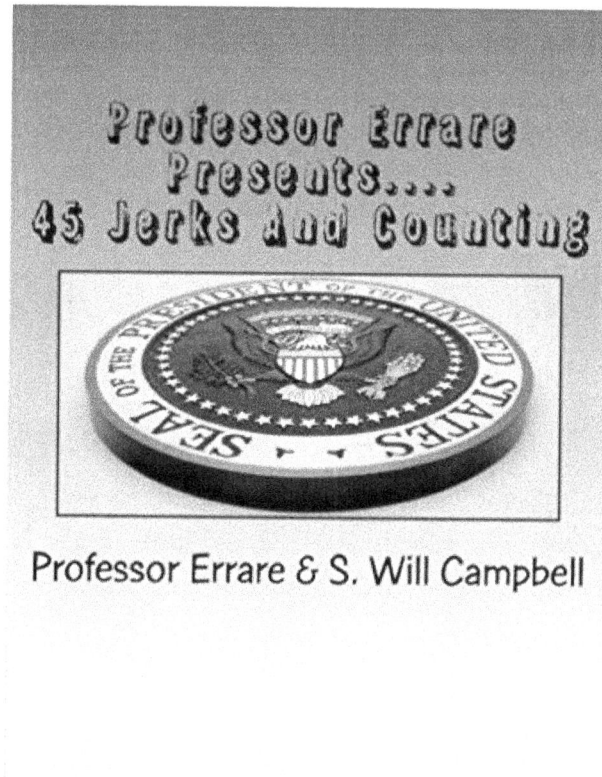

Professor Errare & S. Will Campbell

About The Authors

Professor Errare is a world renowned cynic with a degree in bullshit from the University of None Of Your Damn Business. Professor Errare is a proponent of old school history, where the historian does not let things like facts or other opinions get in the way of a good story. Professor Errare hopes that this book generates some income because you can't get coke and hookers for free. He currently runs a Facebook page by the same name where he provides a weekly dose of knowledge.

Please check out more of Professor Errare at:
http://www.facebook.com/professorerrare

S. Will Campbell has absolutely no interest in history, but he does know how to type, which is a necessity given that Professor Errare lacks this skill. S. Will Campbell wants nothing to do with Professor Errare, but a collection of sleazy photos that could easily get put on the internet keeps him in line. S. Will Campbell's crippling anxiety keeps him from having a wife and kids, or even pets, but he does have a nice house plant named Morton that keeps him company.

www.ingramcontent.com/pod-product-compliance
Lightning Source LLC
Chambersburg PA
CBHW081635040426
42449CB00014B/3318